CW00434299

# HAUNTED
# HALIFAX
## & DISTRICT

# HAUNTED
# HALIFAX
# & DISTRICT

## Kai Roberts

The
History
Press

*To Katie*

First published 2014

The History Press
The Mill, Brimscombe Port
Stroud, Gloucestershire, GL5 2QG
www.thehistorypress.co.uk

© Kai Roberts, 2014

The right of Kai Roberts to be identified as the Author
of this work has been asserted in accordance with the
Copyright, Designs and Patents Act 1988.

All rights reserved. No part of this book may be reprinted
or reproduced or utilised in any form or by any electronic,
mechanical or other means, now known or hereafter invented,
including photocopying and recording, or in any information
storage or retrieval system, without the permission in writing
from the Publishers.
British Library Cataloguing in Publication Data.
A catalogue record for this book is available from the British Library.

ISBN 978 0 7509 6006 9

Typesetting and origination by The History Press
Printed in Great Britain

# CONTENTS

# ACKNOWLEDGEMENTS

THANKS to Cate Ludlow, Naomi Reynolds, Maggie Owens, John Billinglsey, Andy Roberts, Helen Roberts, Phil Roper, Patrick Green, Andy Owens, Stephen Wade, Paul Weatherhead, T. Sutton, Anthea Smith, Jill Kendall, June Kendall, Chelsea Bushby, Steven Robertshaw, Michael Tyler, Malcolm Bull, Carrie Hellyer, Lesley Tudor, Ethel Aked, Ben Marshall, Steven Beasley, Hannah-Rose Little, Helen Burns, Barry Clarke, Christine McOwen, Ann Haigh, Ian Fell, Carol McCambridge, Matt Clay, Tony Nicholson, Jodie Michele, Penny Fell, Brian Wardell, Shaun Parkinson, Anne Marie Tait and the staff of Halifax Central Library Reference Department.

Unless otherwise credited, illustrations are from the author's collection.

# 1

# HALIFAX TOWN CENTRE

### Ghosts of the Halifax Gibbet

In 1622, the poet John Taylor composed 'The Beggars' Litany' and forever preserved the roguish wisdom, 'From Hell, Hull and Halifax, Good Lord deliver us'. In the seventeenth century such miscreants were afraid of Hull on account of its notorious gaol, but Halifax held a worse terror still – the Gibbet Law. By this statute, anybody caught stealing goods worth more than 13½d was condemned to death by decapitation by guillotine: a punishment which had long since been discontinued for such petty crimes elsewhere in the country.

The Gibbet Law stipulated that to condemn a felon to death, the Bailiff of Sowerbyshire must convene a jury of sixteen men to determine the guilt of the defendant. Such tribunals were typically held in Moot Hall near the parish church. If convicted, the prisoner would be held for three days in the stocks before being led to the gibbet. Originally, the device stood closer to the town centre, on Cow Green at the bottom of Gibbet Street, and was only moved further up the hill in 1645.

Moot Hall was a timber-framed building erected around 1274 and later cased in stone. Until its demolition in June 1957, it was with this building that ghosts of the Gibbet's victims were most associated, rather than the site of the machine itself. Local historian, F.A. Leyland, wrote in 1852: 'There are people living who remember, in their childhood, old men saying [how] in times past many [convicted criminals] had been conducted

A replica erected on Gibbet Street in 1974. (Philip Roper)

A plaque marking the site of Moot Hall.

from its portals to the scaffold and that in the long winter nights the misty forms of men without heads might been seen gliding through its gloomy precincts.'

By the twentieth century, Moot Hall was known by the name 'Jackson's Court' – supposedly after a fearsome judge who'd sent many men to the gibbet during his reign of terror and, rather bizarrely, kept a vicious pet weasel. The ghosts of Jackson and his companion were rumoured to haunt the vicinity of Moot Hall, but as their historical existence is entirely apocryphal, such traditions should be treated with caution.

Another apparition associated with the Gibbet Law was produced by one of the statute's more idiosyncratic provisions. Any prisoner on the scaffold who could release themselves from their bonds before the axe fell and make it across the boundary of Halifax township was a free

man – as long as he never returned. As the northern perimeter of Halifax was marked by the Hebble Brook, only 500 yards or so from the gibbet's position, the feat was not impossible and history records that at least two men managed it.

The first man to escape from the gibbet was known simply as Dinnis and the chronological details of his escape are vague. Much more is known about the second – a robber called John Lacey, who evaded the blade in 1617. Lacey was foolish enough to return to Halifax several years later and his exploits had not been forgotten in the town. He was quickly recaptured and the gibbet finally claimed his head on 29 January 1623.

Since 1971, the achievement of Lacey and Dinnis has been commemorated by a pub on Pellon Lane known as The Running Man. It is a utilitarian modern structure and the building it

The sign of The Running Man. (Philip Roper)

replaced was no older than the nineteenth century; nonetheless, the headless ghost of John Lacey is rumoured to have been seen in the establishment. Sadly, details of the sighting are scarce and it may just be a rumour legend inspired by the name of the pub, or even deliberately fabricated by the owners to add further colour.

## The Minster Church of St John the Baptist, Halifax

The parish of Halifax was formerly the largest and richest in England. Although some vestiges of the original twelfth-century church remain within the fabric, the building seen today was mostly constructed between 1437 and 1449; whilst like many medieval churches, Halifax Minster was extensively restored during the Victorian era. The work was undertaken in 1878 on the instructions of Revd Francis Pigou, who described the

church as 'dilapidated, dusty, foul, strewn with human remains, and no better than a charnel house'.

Pigou's account is scarcely surprising. During the eighteenth and nineteenth century, there seems to have been scant respect for burials in the churchyard; many tombstones were stolen for use in the construction of nearby houses and in the 1770s grave robbing was so rife that even the sexton is rumoured to have been involved. There were also a number of clandestine inhumations in this period, given to those refused official burial in consecrated ground.

One such instance occurred following the death of Nan Beverley in 1796; a hawker and prostitute who expired following a drinking binge at her cellar-dwelling in Woolshops. The vicar, Revd Henry William Coulthurst, and sexton, Joseph Binns, were adamant that a fallen woman could not be buried in the churchyard and left her to be interred beside the highway. However, at 4 a.m. the following morning, residents of nearby houses were disturbed by the sound of her family surreptitiously digging a grave for the unfortunate Nan Beverley at the bottom of the churchyard.

The Halifax coat of arms featuring the head of St John the Baptist.

9

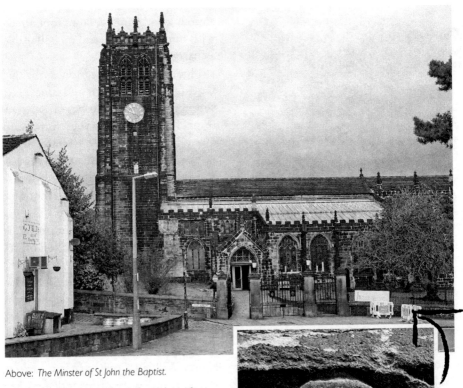

Above: *The Minster of St John the Baptist.*

Right: *An apotropaic stone head carved on Halifax Minster.*

Popular superstition at this time often regarded the spirits of those buried without proper religious ceremony as prime candidates for post-mortem return and as a local writer later noted, 'For many years the children were afraid to stay out late at night lest they should see Nan Beverley, the subject of an unhallowed and clandestine burial'. However, perhaps Nan Beverley's ghost was not merely a nineteenth-century bogeyman used to encourage children to return home when darkness fell; perhaps her restless revenant disturbs the peace of the churchyard still ...

Author Stephen Wade certainly had an uncanny experience whilst exploring the precincts of the churchyard one wintry Sunday evening in 2006. He wrote, 'There was that eerie silence we feel when snow somehow insulates much of the normal sounds around ... I had stopped for a few seconds in the evening twilight, close to the church walls, and I was aware of shuffling sounds from around the corner. It sounded like an animal – the kind of noise dogs might make if snuffling or digging. I walked slowly around to where the noise was coming from, but there was nothing to see – and yet I could still hear the sounds, as if there was something just a few feet from me.'

## The Ring O' Bells Inn, Upper Kirkgate

The Ring O' Bells inn stands in the very shadow of Halifax Minster and if its current name was not enough to denote its ecclesiastic connections, it was formerly known as the Sign of the Church. Although the current building dates to 1720, a hostelry has stood on the site since at least the fifteenth century – no doubt providing for the crowds of pilgrims that once swarmed down Cripplegate to sup the curative waters of St John's Well nearby. The surrounding streets were once the very centre of the medieval town, although by the Industrial Revolution the area was notorious for its slums and rookeries, leading to their demolition in 1890.

*The Ring O' Bells with Halifax Minster in the background.*

Ghostly activity at the pub was brought to public attention in 2007, when licensee Angie Hopkins told the *Halifax Evening Courier* about their resident fireside spook – familiarly dubbed 'Walter'. 'Sometimes people have said they can smell something strong like a pipe being lit and smoked,' she explained, 'I had one customer who came to me just as he was leaving. He said "I've been watching this old chap all night …" It would be lovely to know if he is an old customer or perhaps even a former landlord.'

Mrs Hopkins went on to describe common poltergeist-type activity, such as finding the bathroom taps had turned themselves on during the night or the beer taps had turned themselves off in the cellar. Her subsequent enquires revealed that a previous landlord and former staff had also encountered ghosts on the premises – including 'a lady in old-fashioned clothing … [who] leaves a smell of lavender in her wake'. Hopkins was not fazed by the presence of such phantasmal guests, however. 'I suppose you just get used to it,' she said, 'I don't think they mean us any harm.'

David Glover, an officer of the Halifax Antiquarian Society, wondered if the haunting was connected to one of the pub's most curious features: an old gravestone cemented into a recess in the cellar. Dated July 1667, the slab commemorates the death of 3-year-old Hannah Priestley of Northowram. Glover also suggested that the stone's position – in the corner closest to the Minster – suggests it may once have sealed a subterranean passage between the two buildings. Rumours of such tunnels have circulated since the eighteenth century, when the pub provided accommodation for the clerks and sextons of the church.

## Square Chapel & Congregational Church, Talbot Square

These two Halifax landmarks dominate the north side of the Piece Hall and their history is intimately connected. The red-brick Square Independent Chapel – the oldest of the two buildings – was designed

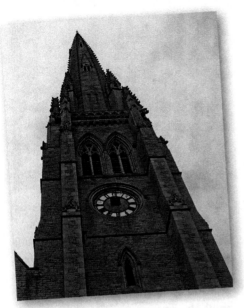

Square Congregation church, Talbot Square.

by the 19-year-old architect Thomas Bradley, two years before he worked on the Piece Hall. When it opened on 24 May 1772, it enjoyed the distinction of being both the first dedicated Independent chapel in Yorkshire, and the largest Nonconformist place of worship in Britain.

Seventy-five years later, the Independent movement in Halifax had grown large and wealthy, and the imposing Square Congregational church was constructed alongside the chapel to accommodate their increasing numbers. Built during the Victorian Gothic Revival, its teetering 235ft spire was once the second tallest in the county. The church opened on 15 July 1857, after which the old neighbouring chapel functioned as a church hall and Sunday school.

As congregations dwindled through the twentieth century, both buildings fell on hard times. Square Congregational church closed its doors in 1970 and barely a year later a fire gutted much of

its fabric. The remaining shell was eventually demolished in 1976, leaving only the Grade II★ listed spire to posterity.

Square Independent Chapel, meanwhile, had been requisitioned by the army during the Second World War and stood derelict for many decades thereafter. Calderdale Council sold it to a charitable organisation in 1989 for a nominal sum of £25, and following extensive restoration, it reopened in 1992 as Square Chapel Centre for the Arts – now a local institution.

In 2005, the remains of Square church required extensive restoration work due to the danger from crumbling masonry and it was at this time that the alleged hauntings in the area came to light. When work on the repairs was arrested in March by the discovery of a mating pair of kestrels (a protected species) nesting in the spire, the council sent a crew of steeplejacks to photograph the birds for an official report.

However, one of the resulting images appeared to capture more than just a nest. Foreman Barry Done explained, 'I was gobsmacked when I printed the photos. We'd been trying to get shots of the birds, but then this eerie figure appeared on one of them … In my twenty years as a steeplejack I've never seen the like.'

The photograph in question was taken by 18-year-old apprentice, Anthony Finnigan, and whilst he claimed not to have seen anything unusual in the spire at the time, he was subsequently reported as being too unnerved by the picture to continue working in the church alone.

Finnigan's image was certainly more compelling than many modern alleged spirit photographs – which are rarely more than examples of pareidolia – and appeared to show a robed figure floating in the spire, its hands raised in a gesture of devotion. However, as local author Paul Weatherhead noted in his discussion of the case, it is suspicious that the original file had been deleted from the camera, meaning it could not be compared with the print.

Following reports in the *Halifax Evening Courier*, a local self-professed medium called Linda Francis came forward with photos taken at an event at the Square Chapel in 1998, which she claimed offered further evidence of ghostly activity in the vicinity. This image appeared to capture a spectral figure with a staff, hunched over another member of the audience and whilst the figure looked suspiciously like an overexposure, Mrs Francis claimed the photograph had been independently analysed and 'signs of camera malfunction, light influx, fogging [or] deliberate hoax' ruled out.

There have also been reports of supernatural activity in surrounding buildings, such as the former premises of Pennine Arts on Blackledge, a cobbled street which runs behind the Square Chapel. A joiner who worked in the property during the summer of 1972 vividly recalls that he and his fellow contractors were mystified by the distinct sound of footsteps coming from an empty upper room.

Linda Francis believed that the presence haunting the buildings around Talbot Square could be identified as Dr John Favour, the Vicar of Halifax from 1593 to 1623 – especially as the pose of the figure in Anthony Finnigan's photograph from Square church closely resembled a bust of Dr Favour in Halifax Minster.

It is true that this strictly Puritan cleric had a bloody reputation; he often took part in the trials and execution of

*Square Congregational Chapel, Talbot Square.*

Catholic recusants at York, including that of the Jesuit martyr, Henry Walpole, in 1595. However, he was incumbent at the old parish church and died 150 years before even the Square Chapel was built, so there seems no reason for him to haunt those buildings; unless it was an expression of his continued displeasure at the 'new and late upstart heresies' those buildings represented!

## The Piece Hall, Halifax

Possibly the jewel in Halifax's crown, the Piece Hall was originally built between 1774 and 1779 to serve as a cloth hall for the district's ever-expanding domestic woollen industry. The vast edifice was built on land known as Talbot Close and housed 315 merchant's lock-ups – all with the same dimensions – from which trade was conducted; while smaller concerns were permitted to sell their wares in the courtyard below.

As the cottage cloth trade declined, the Piece Hall's original function was soon redundant. It was reopened in 1871 as a market hall and later narrowly avoided proposals by the local authority to demolish the building in the 1960s.

The Piece Hall was extensively redeveloped in 1976. In addition to housing an art gallery and museum, the former merchants lock-ups were converted into retail while the courtyard was used for a flea market and concert events. As town centre retail waned in the twenty-first century, Calderdale Council sought new ways to make it profitable and the Piece Hall closed in early 2014 for yet another major redevelopment.

It is hardly surprising that a building thronged with so many lives over the centuries has been populated with its fair share of otherworldly tenants. The most commonly referenced is the ghost of a small girl variously named Amy, Mary or Abigail; although it's unclear whether these are different girls or simply different shopkeepers' names for the same spirit – the latter seems most probable.

Her presence was most often noticed in a shop on the upper gallery which sold jewellery, gemstones and minerals. The owners never saw her phantom

*The interior of Halifax Piece Hall. (W. Burgess)*

directly, but often caught glimpses in their peripheral vision, and she was blamed for moving items round in the display cabinets – even sometimes causing them to vanish altogether.

Her activity extended to neighbouring shops on the top tier. These included a book shop – in which she threw volumes from the shelves during the night – and a sweetshop, whose owners so pitied the unfortunate mite they left a lollipop out for her each night. They believed that, although she was a mischievous ghost, she was not malevolent and welcomed her to their shop. Such an offering recalls the libation of milk many rural farmers used to leave out on the hearth overnight for household faeries such as boggarts.

The Piece Hall ghost is generally identified with one of the girls from the Halifax Workhouse, which until 1840 was situated on Upper Kirkgate nearby. This grim institution opened in 1635 to house the 'undeserving' or 'idle' poor of the parish and provide them with meaningful activity – which essentially meant forced labour between 5 a.m. and 8 p.m. In 1777 it accommodated over 100 inmates whom the workhouse guardians hired out to local businesses. Perhaps that's how the girl's connection with the Piece Hall came about.

Other ghosts are rumoured to haunt the Piece Hall, although none are as widely attested as the spectral girl. One of the staircases is said to be inhabited by the lingering shade of a cloth merchant who died when a scuffle between rival traders escalated. The extensive cellars – which are primarily used for storage by the council – are also supposed to have an uncanny atmosphere and spiritualist mediums claim to have made contact with presences in their depths.

An anonymous apparition is also alleged to rattle the locked gates. But, whilst the Piece Hall used to shut at 6 p.m. every evening and reopen at 9 a.m., at the time of writing the current renovation programme is projected to last eighteen months from January 2014 – hence the gates will only be opened to allow works traffic access and the phantom gate-rattler may be shaking their chains for some considerable time.

## The Old Cock Inn, Southgate

This ancient building was originally built as a private home around 1580, possibly by Sir Henry Savile, a local scholar and associate of the celebrated Elizabethan magus, Dr John Dee. Since it was converted into a tavern in 1688, the building witnessed a number of significant episodes in the history of the town. It was a favoured spot of Branwell Brontë, drunkard brother of Charlotte, Emily and Anne, who often ran up large debts in the bar; whilst the elaborately decorated Oak Room upstairs provided an assembly hall for numerous civic societies, including West Yorkshire's oldest Masonic Lodge and the Loyal Georgean Society, whose meeting on 23 December 1852 ultimately led to the foundation of the Halifax Building Society.

The paranormal incidents were recorded in the autobiography of Revd Thomas Wright, who also wrote the earliest history of the district, *The Antiquities of the Town of Halifax* in Yorkshire, in 1738. Wright explains that his 'half-aunt', Martha Horton, was landlady at the Old Cock for over thirty years, and it was to this venerable lady that the ghosts appeared.

*The Old Cock Inn, Southgate.*

stayed at the inn appeared one night in the bar 'looking earnestly at her through the railings' around the same hour at which she later heard he had died. This type of ghost – the wraith of a distant loved one seen at the moment of their death – is known as a 'crisis apparition'. The notion was popular amongst clergymen such as Thomas Wright in the seventeenth and eighteenth century, as it seemed to offer evidence of the soul's survival after death and was often recorded as exemplar in theological tracts. However, crisis apparitions are usually discrete manifestations and there have been no reports to suggest their presence lingered at the Old Cock.

To quote Wright's account in full: 'After the death of her first husband she [Martha] married a Nathaniel Longbottom, who proved but a very indifferent husband, deserted her, and went to London, married a second wife during her lifetime, used to send threatening letters to extort money from her, etc. She told me she saw his apparition the night of his death, as she lay awake with a Mr Newton, with whom she lived at that time and who was fast asleep by her side; that she looked earnestly at the ghost for some time, and it looked as earnestly at her … She told her bedfellow in the morning that Nathaniel was dead, she had seen him in the night, and expected a letter with an account of his death by the next post, which happened according to her expectations.'

Horton had a second similar experience some years later, when the apparition of a maltster who often

## The Palace Theatre, Ward's End

Constructed during the harsh winter of 1902–3, the Palace became affectionately known as the 'sweetest theatre in the north', as sugar was added to the mortar to prevent it from freezing in the subzero temperatures. Following its grand opening on 30 July 1903, the Palace became one of the most popular theatres in Halifax; during its lifetime, it attracted some of the biggest music-hall and variety acts in the country, including the likes of Harry Houdini, Charlie Chaplin, George Formby, Arthur Askey, Gracie Fields, Sandy Powell and Little Tich.

It also hosted many smaller stars – now mostly forgotten – who were the bread and butter of the vaudeville circuit, such as the Lancastrian comedian, Clarence 'Tubby' Turner. This rotund gentleman regularly had audiences at the Palace rolling in the aisles with his stuttering

*The site of the Palace Theatre at Ward's End.*

catchphrase 'If it's h-h-okay with you, it's h-h-okay with me!' and a slapstick sketch that involved getting hopelessly entangled in a deckchair he was attempting to erect – which only goes to prove L.P. Hartley's famous assertion, 'The past is a foreign country; they do things differently there.'

Perhaps afraid that he would forever be remembered as that 'Little Fat Chap in New Absurdities', Turner penned his first play at the age of 60. Tragically, however, he never lived to see the début performance of *Summat For Nowt*. On 19 January 1952, the variety-show veteran collapsed midway through his deckchair routine at the Palace Theatre in Halifax and passed away two days later in St John's Hospital on Gibbet Street.

The popularity of music hall was waning by the 1950s and, in the period after Turner's death, management at the Palace attempted to boost dwindling ticket sales by introducing repertory theatre to the bill. Although there were residencies by distinguished touring companies such as Harry Hanson's Court Players, the Palace also began to put on shows by local amateur dramatic societies – one of which decided to present Clarence Turner's *Summat For Nowt*, doubtless as a tribute to its late author, whose career had ended so abruptly on that very stage.

According to the ghost-lore collector, Terence Williams, during one of these performances a young actress in the cast 'dried up' mid-scene. Unable to recall the remainder of her dialogue, she glanced in panic to the wings, but rather than the regular stagehand in the prompt corner, she saw an unfamiliar face mouthing the lines to her – seemingly without reference to a script.

After the curtain had fallen, the actress was unable to find her mysterious ally to thank. She began making inquiries as to his identity, but evidently none of her fellow players had noticed anybody incongruous backstage. It is not clear how she arrived at her ultimate discovery: she might have seen a photograph or her description might have prompted somebody's memory. However, it seems the woman was left in no doubt that the figure she'd seen in the wings was none other than Clarence 'Tubby' Turner himself.

If the ghost of the portly entertainer did haunt the scene of his last hurrah, he did not have a chance to lurk in the shadows beyond the footlights for long. Repertory theatre failed to arrest dwindling audience numbers and the Palace closed its doors on 30 May 1959. The building was demolished the following year and its former location at the corner of Southgate and Horton Street is now occupied by a concrete block of commercial properties.

## The Old Picture House, Ward's End

A familiar sight on the corner of Ward's End in Halifax town centre's 'theatre quarter', for many years this building has housed two popular (and occasionally notorious) nightclubs – Liquid (formerly the Coliseum) and Maine Street. However, it was originally designed as the town's first purpose-built cinema, the Picture House, which opened on 20 October 1913 to much fanfare.

It survived in this role until 1962, when it reopened as the Top Rank Bingo & Social Club, before enjoying a second wind as the Astra cinema between 1973 and 1982. The building embraced its present function as a provincial fleshpot in 1987, since which time its fortunes have been relatively consistent.

In October 2008 (suspiciously close to Hallowe'en), staff reported a number of supernatural incidents at the venue, including encounters with the apparition of a young man with 'tousled hair' wearing 'black trousers and a crumpled

white shirt', which left some employees afraid to work upstairs on their own.

According to manager, Neill Maguire, 'It was 4 a.m. on Sunday, I was doing the stock take upstairs in the Maine Street bar when I saw someone. I thought it was a customer who'd got lost because downstairs was still open … So I walked towards him and that's when he walked through the wall.' Barman Philip Pearcy added, 'I saw him a few weeks ago … He was stood watching me but when I went over to speak to him he disappeared and all the fridges started shutting.'

Following the report in the *Halifax Evening Courier*, the newspaper was contacted by 68-year-old Moira Gurteen and 63-year-old Anne Wells, who'd worked in the building during its term as a bingo hall. Both claimed that an identical apparition had been witnessed in the 1960s. 'It was well known among staff that there was a ghost,' Mrs Gurteen said, 'but you didn't say anything except to each other. You didn't want to be ridiculed.'

Meanwhile, Mrs Wells had no doubt that the spectre encountered by Neil Macguire and Philip Pearcy was the same figure she'd seen between 1962 and 1964. 'It's his hair', she explained, 'It's exactly the same style.' The women added that he would often be seen on the balcony – which at the time was unused – watching the bingo-players below.

All four witnesses agreed that the ghost they'd seen bore a striking resemblance to the photograph of a young man taken six decades earlier. The subject of the portrait was a 25 year old named Raymond Farrar, who'd once worked as a projectionist at the Picture House, having picked up the trade serving with the Entertainments National Service Association during

*Liquid and Maine Street, formerly the Picture House at Ward's End.*

the Second World War. On 9 April 1948 – only seven weeks after his wife had given birth to their daughter – Mr Farrar was trapped in the projection room as a blaze tore through the Picture House. Out of 600 people in the cinema at time, only Farrar failed to make it out alive. The film he'd been showing when the fire broke out was Universal Studios' classic 1942 B-movie, *The Ghost of Frankenstein.*

## The Royal Oak, Ward's End

Although its mock-Tudor frontage has led many to believe that the Royal Oak is one of the town's more venerable taverns, the present building is no older than 1931. It was erected by Ramsden's Brewery on the site of an eighteenth-century coaching inn of the same name, using timber salvaged from a steam

frigate which had served the British Navy between 1860 and 1888 under the title, HMS *Newcastle.*

In 2012, Dean Majors complained that he'd observed a variety of poltergeist-type phenomena in the year since he'd taken on the Royal Oak's license. His experiences were typical of many pub-based hauntings: glasses flying off their shelves; cellar lights switching themselves on or off; essentially all low-level effects of a primarily kinetic nature. Perhaps more substantially, on one occasion Majors claimed to have seen an entire barrel levitate from the ground.

From conversations with old regulars, the new landlord learnt that local tradition credited the establishment with three distinct ghosts. Most notable is the spectre of an unknown woman wearing seventeenth-century Puritan or Quaker dress, who had been vividly witnessed by a customer around forty years earlier.

*Dirty Dick's, formerly the Royal Oak at Ward's End.*

The second presence was imagined to belong to the son of the last landlord of the original pub, prior to its demolition in 1929. This unfortunate young man is supposed to have burned to death when a sparking ember from the hearth set his clothes alight. Unfortunately, this story lacks documentary confirmation – much like that of the pub's third otherworldly resident, whose history is connected not with the pub, but with the ship from which it was built.

HMS *Newcastle* travelled the globe extensively during its twenty-eight years in commission, but its biography is rather less distinguished than some other vessels to have sailed under that name. Although it was armed with thirty-one guns, this warship was never actually involved in any conflicts; as a member of the Flying Squadron with the East Indies Station its purpose was primarily for display. It sailed the South Pacific and Indian Ocean as a reminder of Britain's naval superiority and to show that the government would protect the country's trading interests in those areas.

As such, the HMS *Newcastle*'s maritime career does not seem to provide much justification for the endurance of an unquiet spirit. However, after it was decommissioned in 1888, the ship was relinquished to the War Department and spent several decades thereafter anchored at HMNB Devonport as a powder-hulk – essentially a nautical warehouse used to store gunpowder away from important facilities on land.

Hence, the Royal Oak's third ghost is supposed to be the spirit of some unfortunate seaman who was fatally injured when the ordnance he was moving aboard HMS *Newcastle* exploded. Whilst accidents of that nature undoubtedly occurred on powder-hulks, in the absence of an official record detailing such an incident in connection with HMS *Newcastle* or HMNB Devonport, it is best regarded as apocryphal.

## Halifax County Court, Prescott Street

For many centuries, justice in Halifax was administered by the Manor of Wakefield. However, when the town was incorporated to become the Borough of Halifax in 1848, the manor court was superseded by a new county court. Initially this was located at Central Hall in Union Street, but on 23 September 1873 the court moved into a new purpose-built home on Prescott Street and for the next century the West Riding Petty Sessions shared the premises with the Halifax division of the West Riding Police Force.

This all changed again during the municipal restructuring of the 1970s; the Prescott Street site continued to house the civil courts and registry office for a while, but it was eventually sold off in the 1990s. During this transition, the building stood vacant for some time and a property surveyor called Jonathan Wilson was responsible for showing prospective buyers around the premises. In his line of work, he was quite used to spending time alone in empty buildings. However, Mr Wilson later told the *Halifax Evening Courier* that the old county court had been a different matter altogether.

He said he often encountered cold-spots in the building, which would fill him with a sense of 'dread, gloom and depression', and ensured that he spent as little time there as possible. Even more curiously, although he had supposedly been given keys to all the doors in the building, he was unable to find one which matched the mechanism on the iron gate which led to the old holding cells. On several occasions he found the gate locked and impossible to budge; yet when he returned later, it had mysteriously opened.

Wilson's uncanny experiences at Prescott Street were shared by a joiner

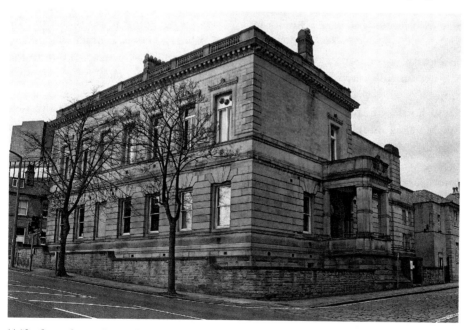

*Halifax County Court on Prescott Street.*

who had been contracted to board up all possible access points to deter squatters and vandals. As he was working on the main doorway – the last available entrance – he grew very conscious of the sound of footsteps in the corridor beyond. They grew closer and closer, yet no figure appeared. The joiner was so convinced he had heard something that he conducted a final inspection of the building to ensure nobody had got shut in. When no intruder revealed themselves, he finished the job and left the place as quickly as he possibly could.

These reports encouraged local paranormal investigator, Andy Owens, to further research the reputation of the building. He was subsequently contacted by a number of former policemen and administrative staff who'd been stationed at Prescott Street over the years. Alan Paley, who'd worked there as a relief clerk in the 1970s, claimed he could think of at least twenty people who'd experienced strange phenomena at Prescott Street, suggesting that the haunting had been active for several decades during the twentieth century.

At least two reports closely matched the account of Jonathan Wilson. Paley himself recalled that often when he was sat at his desk in the General Office, 'a sudden inexplicable chill would surge through the room and fill you with a strange, eerie feeling'. Meanwhile, another retired officer – who preferred to remain anonymous – told Owens that he had once been inspecting the cells at the end of a shift when the iron gate slammed firmly shut, trapping him in the empty vault. Unable to attract anybody's attention, he was forced to squeeze out through a tiny window.

Paley also explained that during his tenure at Prescott Street, the general office housed some very antiquated apparatus for internal communications – including a bell board linked to the cells below and a speaking-tube which connected with the magistrates' clerks' offices on the floor above. If prisoners wished to contact the general office, they rang the bell; whilst the magistrates' clerks would blow a whistle attached to the speaking tube. Paley claimed that both the bells and whistle regularly sounded during the night-shift when the cells and offices were unoccupied, and an inspection confirmed that no human presence could have operated the devices.

## Wainhouse Tower, King Cross

Another of the district's most distinctive landmarks, Wainhouse Tower stands 275ft high, making it the tallest folly in the world. The structure took four years to build and was completed on 9 September 1875. Its octagonal tower is crowned by an elaborate cupola, beneath which there is a viewing platform, accessible to the public only after a climb of 403 steps on designated open days.

Surprisingly, although Wainhouse Tower has long been perceived as the embodiment of the enmity between John Wainhouse and his rival Sir Henry Edwards, it is not their ghosts who are associated with the folly. Rather it is the ghost of a young woman, who is seen weeping in the grounds at the foot of the tower; murmuring, 'They done for him ...' to herself over and over again. Often she is not seen and only her pitiful sobs are heard.

According to local folklore collected by Stephen Wade in 2006, her story could be traced to the home front in the Second World War. During the conflict, American servicemen were stationed at Wellesley Barracks in Pellon and – as so often happened – a number of local girls started stepping out with the GIs. These liaisons were bitterly resented by local men and the simmering tension between them soon erupted.

One evening, a Halifax woman and her GI sweetheart were rendezvousing in the cemetery at the foot of the tower when they were set upon by a gang of local thugs. The girl was forced to watch as they beat the blameless American to within an inch of his life, and she was so traumatised by witnessing the brutal assault – especially as she blamed herself – that she was confined to a psychiatric hospital until her death in 1974.

It is not clear to what extent we should regard this story as accurate; although anybody familiar with the psychoge-ography of King Cross and Pellon may find the narrative horribly possible. If the tradition is apocryphal, it may be stitched together from a variety of motifs appro-priated from popular media sources; yet it may also personify a memory of the local mood during Halifax's time as a garrison town in the Second World War – valuable social history at least.

*Wainhouse Tower, King Cross.*

# 2

# NORTH HALIFAX

## Dean Clough Mills, Stannary

Another Halifax landmark, the industrial history of Dean Clough really begins in 1802 when John Crossley leased a textile mill on the banks of the Hebble Brook to produce carpets. The enterprise grew steadily and, by the time of Crossley's death in 1837, it employed 300 people. His family continued the business under the name of John Crossley & Sons Ltd, embarking on a programme of expansion from 1841–69 which produced the imposing industrial complex that stands today. During this period, eleven mills were constructed; covering 40 acres with 1¼ million sq.ft of factory space. It became the world's largest carpet factory and by the end of the century, it employed 5,000 people in Halifax alone.

With the decline of British manufacturing in the second half of the twentieth century, the profitability of the mills dwindled and Crossley's Carpets pulled out of Halifax in 1983. However, in contrast to the fate of so many other former factory sites in Calderdale, Dean Clough only thrived and is today regarded as a paragon of successful industrial regeneration. Redeveloped as a centre for arts, business and light industry, the complex now houses the offices of around 150 companies; plus conference facilities, retails outlets, several art galleries, a number of restaurants, a prestigious theatre, a hotel, a radio station and a cookery school.

Otherworldly activity at Dean Clough has primarily been reported from F Mill, formerly used for flax spinning but now an administrative centre for NHS Calderdale, and D Mill, arguably the centrepiece of the complex, housing the Crossley Gallery, Design House Restaurant and Viaduct Theatre. In recent years, D Mill has hosted the annual Halifax Ghost Story Festival and whilst this event is devoted to supernatural fiction, the suitability of the venue is doubtless enhanced by the fact it can boast its own spectral traditions.

Such is D Mill's reputation that an investigation into paranormal phenomena carried out there in March 2006 was filmed and broadcast live as part of the Living TV series *Derek Acorah's Ghost Towns*. Although programmes of this kind represent one of the vehicles through which supernatural folklore is

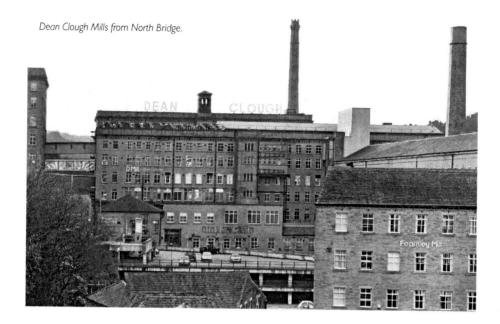

*Dean Clough Mills from North Bridge.*

transmitted in the present era and serve as passable entertainment, they should not be mistaken for legitimate study or a source of reliable information. In fact, even the independent ghost-hunting team who Ruggie Media contracted to carry out the investigation at Dean Clough subsequently expressed concern regarding the ethics and credibility of the broadcast programme.

Nonetheless, a number of people working in the complex have reported witnessing apparitions over the years. David Nesbitt, a media spokesman for Dean Clough Ltd, told the press that whilst he had not seen anything himself, he had heard many rumours during his twelve years working there. As with so many Victorian industrial buildings, the stories most often pertain to the spirits of children once forced to toil there by the cruel and rapacious factory system – almost as if they're a personification of our collective guilt. During the nineteenth century, child labour was certainly exploited at Dean Clough and the records of John Crossley & Sons Ltd contain numerous registers of the 'young persons' employed there. It took more than a century of legislation to finally bring the practice to an end.

A supervisor at the Design House Restaurant told the local press, 'Throughout the three years I've worked here there has always been some creepy presence. Staff noticed a little boy they think is about 7 years old, walking around the building. One evening I was working late with a colleague when we noticed the reflection of a little boy in the mirror running towards the toilet. We went inside to find nothing there.' There were also reports of a spectral girl loitering around the restaurant, and like so many ghosts observed by employees of the hospitality industry, these spooks have been blamed for all manner of occupational irritations, from shattering glasses to fiddling with the electrics.

The researcher Stephen Wade has also collected reports of a phantom suicide on North Bridge, which carries a road into the town centre over Hebble Brook as it runs through Dean Clough. A bridge has been recorded here since the thirteenth century, but the present double-arched iron structure was erected in 1871. With a vertiginous height of 75ft at its central point, it has been the scene of a number of suicides over the years. Stephen Wade believed the apparition reported to him may be identified as Benjamin Dowse, an employee of Crossley's Carpets who suffered from 'congestion of the lungs' and threw himself from the parapet of North Bridge in April 1878. Tragically, the fall did not kill him outright and he suffered the agony of his injuries for some time before he finally expired.

## Long Can, Ovenden Wood

Originally a fourteenth-century timber-framed building cased in stone, Long Can was substantially rebuilt in 1637 by James Murgatroyd (who was also responsible for Kershaw House at Luddenden and East Riddlesden Hall near Keighley). A private residence for much of its history, it was purchased and restored by Webster's Fountain Head Brewery in 1985 to house their visitors' centre, including hospitality suites and a museum.

Unfortunately, Webster's Brewery closed in 1996 with the loss of several hundred jobs. Much of the former site was redeveloped for housing, but as a listed building, Long Can remained untouched. It stood derelict for a time but was converted into a successful pub and restaurant in 2009.

Local paranormal investigator, Andy Owens, first documented the haunting at Long Can in the 1990s. The connection between structural alterations and supernatural activity is a common theme in contemporary ghost lore and indeed strange phenomena was first observed at the hall following its renovation in 1986.

Owens spoke to Sarah Thornton, a former catering manageress who had often heard slamming doors and mysterious footsteps when she was working alone on the upper floor, preparing the VIP suites for guests. Ms Thornton also reported the experience of a waitress

Long Can, Ovenden Wood.

*Fold Farm, also known as Mixenden Old Hall.*

who'd been browsing the museum during her break, when she turned to see 'an elderly lady in a long grey dress who appeared to be falling downwards, as if through the floorboards'.

The waitress's encounter was corroborated by cleaner Betty Greenwood, who'd seen a 'white, opaque object' drift past her and melt through the cellar door. Staff also reported sudden temperature drops and a sensation of being observed by some incorporeal presence. One cleaner even felt herself tapped on the shoulder by a disembodied hand.

Andy Owens also interviewed Harold Maude, who had worked as the host at Long Can Visitor Centre. Maude recalled an occasion on which he'd discovered a number of artefacts in one of the display cases moved from the top shelf and neatly rearranged at the bottom. The museum had been closed for two days over a bank holiday and he was certain the exhibit had not been in that state when he left it. The only other person with a key to

the cabinet was the security guard, who denied having touched anything.

It may be significant that the objects moved included a number of old shoes discovered in the walls of Long Can during renovation. Such items were often placed in the fabric of buildings up until the nineteenth century, and although the purpose of this custom is still debated, the most widely accepted hypothesis is that the shoes were supposed to protect the house against evil spirits – possibly inspired by legends in which holy men conjure the Devil into an old boot.

## Fold Farm, Illingworth

Sometimes referred to as Mixenden Old Hall, the fabric of Fold Farm includes remnants of the original timber-framed aisled house built around 1450. It was cased in stone during the fifteenth century, possibly around 1525 when the church of St Mary the Virgin was first established at Illingworth. In 1925, the incumbent of St Mary's, Revd George Oakley, privately published a history of the church which speculated on a link between its foundation and a grisly tradition associated with Fold Farm.

The legend has a number of variants but they all agree that the events took place before there was a church at Illingworth, meaning the residents of Fold Farm were forced to travel to Halifax every Sunday to worship. They left a maid behind at the hall attending to the kitchens and a little while after her employers had set out, she was disturbed by a knock on the scullery door.

The maid was confronted by the sight of a weary traveller in desperate need of food and shelter. In some versions, the caller is disguised as an old woman, in others he is merely an exhausted wayfarer. As the rules of hospitality dictated in this period, the maid invited the traveller inside and sat them by the fire whilst she prepared some food.

However, as the maid cooked she noticed that something was amiss with her guest. Perhaps she observed the brace of pistols concealed at his waist or the hairy muscular arms beneath the folds of the dress. Either way, she realised with horror that she had granted access to a highwayman and knew that if she did not act soon he would rob the house and possibly rape or murder her.

Thus, the maid took a pan of simmering fat from the range and flung it in the intruder's face. One version of the story suggests the scalding fat killed him, but another claims that it only enraged the villain, and the family returned to find a pillaged house and the corpse of their servant. In a further variant, it was not a maid who was left in the house but an elderly relative who was too frail to travel and met a similar end to the maid at the hands of a ruthless highwayman.

Revd Oakley suggested that the tragedy led the occupants of Fold Farm to raise money for the foundation of a church at Illingworth, so they never had to leave their property unattended for so long again. However, the historical veracity of the tradition is dubious. Although Illingworth would've been an isolated spot in the sixteenth century and easy pickings for the cunning thief, the story associated with Fold Farm is a migratory legend told about many old houses across the country – including Newhouse Hall at Sheepridge near Huddersfield.

Nonetheless, the legend has bestowed a number of ghosts upon Fold Farm, the identity of which largely depends on which variant of the narrative the teller accepts. Locals in the early twentieth century believed it was the spectre of the highwayman himself, or the elderly relative, whose apparition appeared in a rocking chair in the parlour.

Yet Christopher Stead, who occupied one partition of Fold Farm in 1977, told the *Halifax Evening Courier* it was the murdered maid who haunted the hall, and claimed his mother-in-law had often seen a phantom girl wearing an apron sat at the bottom of the stairs. This belief was repeated to researcher Stephen Wade in 2008 by Eileen and John Nicholls, so it may be the dominant version of the legend today. Whether it is anything more than a legend remains a moot point.

# Holdsworth House, Holmfield

When an artist of George Harrison's stature asks if your home is haunted, it is to be hoped you have a stimulating reply. Fortunately 14-year-old Gail Moss should have been able to satisfy Harrison's curiosity when he asked her that question on the morning of 10 October 1964, as Holdsworth House does indeed have a reputation for being haunted and Harrison had just spent the night in the very room the ghost most often frequents.

The previous evening, the Beatles had played a gig in Bradford and returned to sleep at the sixteenth-century hall – at that time known as the Cavalier Country Club and owned by Gail's parents. Whilst John Lennon and Ringo Starr slept in a room now used as an office, Paul McCartney and George shared what is currently called the Ayrton Room.

The Ayrton Room was originally the main bedchamber at Holdsworth House and since the building was converted into a hotel by Freddie and Rita Pearson in 1963 it has served as a luxury suite for guests. A number of visitors have reported seeing a 'white lady' type apparition in the room, although the figure has recently been observed by diners in the restaurant below, whilst staff have experienced the sensation of being watched and other intimations of incorporeal presence in rooms throughout this ancient building.

The Holdsworth family name is first recorded at Holmfield in 1272 and documents show that a timber-framed house was built there by William Holdsworth in 1435. A carving of a Maltese cross survives from this period on the east gable of Holdsworth House, indicating that during the Middle Ages the estate paid rent to the Order of Knights of St John of Jersusalem, also known as the Knights Hospitaller – one of the most famous religio-military orders of the Crusades.

The hall seen today was built around 1633 for Abraham Briggs – a colourful

*Holdsworth House at Holmfield.*

Ovenden Hall.

character who subsequently drank or gambled away his fortune and sold Holdsworth House in 1657 to buy a tavern in Halifax. The Nonconformist preacher and diarist, Revd Oliver Heywood, records that Briggs was 'a nightly drinker, usually called amongst them "Prevailed" for a nickname' and met his death 'having drunk much, fed excessively' in 1671.

Briggs sold Holdsworth House to Henry Wadsworth, whose descendants dwelt at the hall for the next 200 years. The Wadsworth family remain strongly associated with the hall historically and the 'white lady' apparition has been identified as Elizabeth Wadsworth who died there on 5 April 1837, aged 77. A noted philanthropist, she was dubbed the 'Lady Bountiful of Holdsworth, Bradshaw and Illingworth' in local memory.

Miss Wadsworth never married and upon her death left the estate to a distant relative called Matthew Ayrton – on the condition that he and all his heirs took the Wadsworth surname. Should they refuse this stipulation, an entail in her will ensured that their inheritance

would be forfeit. Evidently she was keen to preserve her family's connection with Holdsworth House and ensure that her own presence was felt there long after her death. If the white lady who haunts the hall today is truly the spirit of Elizabeth Wadsworth, she has achieved such intentions in more ways than one.

Another tenacious old lady determined to remain in her family home was once believed to haunt Ovenden Hall nearby. This ancient pile on Ovenden Road was locally known as the 'haunted house' for many years and its resident spectre identified with Frances Norton, who'd taken up residence there in 1713 when she married Captain John Furness – grandson of the man who'd built the hall fifty years earlier.

Frances was unfortunate enough to outlive both Captain Furness, and her second husband – the uniquely monikered Gabetis Norton – but she tenanted Ovenden Hall until her death on 3 July 1770, aged 88. As local historian W.B. Trigg, observed, 'She must have dearly loved its old grey face … for there was a persistent tradition that her spirit could often be seen gliding along the old corridors and flitting about the panelled rooms'.

Writing in 1925, Trigg noted that 'even yet there are those who declare they have seen her shadowy form' which suggests reports of the apparition persisted well into the twentieth century. The memory of her presence seems to have been lost when the hall was converted for business use around 1944. At the time of writing, however, Ovenden Hall stands empty and derelict, so perhaps the local imagination populates its precincts with ghosts once more.

## Two Hilltop Hostelries, Wainstalls

Shortly after Terry Pinder took over the license of the Delvers' Arms at Wainstalls in 2008, regular customers started to ask if he'd yet encountered the ghost. At first, Pinder was sceptical and assumed the regulars were merely joking with a new landlord. However, over the following six months, he experienced persistent phenomena exhibiting all the hallmarks of a pub poltergeist.

He later told the *Halifax Evening Courier*:

> I was sitting upstairs after closing when I heard a loud crashing noise ... When I came downstairs I saw a glass on the floor some 6ft away from the shelf. It was still intact. I could not understand how this happened. I have tried so many times to replicate it and every time the glass broke.

Subsequently, Mr Pinder and several customers observed three glasses swinging on their hooks above the bar for over an hour, although there was no breeze or vibration and none of the other glasses were moving.

The history of the Delvers' Arms is relatively undistinguished or much has passed undocumented. It was built in the 1820s as Oddfellows Arms and traded as the New Delight Inn for many years, before adopting its current title in 1987.

*The Delvers' Arms at Wainstalls.*

The former Withens Hotel on the
road from Wainstalls to Oxenhope.

Little else is known and there certainly seems to be nothing to justify the pub's reputation for being haunted.

However, perhaps the Delvers' Arms has inherited a homeless spectre from the former Withens Hotel nearby. Located 1,392ft above sea level on the lonely road over the hills to Oxenhope, the Withens Hotel opened in 1864 and became famous as the highest pub in West Yorkshire. A millennium beacon was lit there on New Year's Eve 1999, but only a couple of years later, the building was badly damaged by fire and never reopened.

In addition to its altitude, the Withens Hotel was also known for two slightly morbid features during its lifetime. The first is a gravestone in an adjacent field inscribed with the epitaph:

Here lie the remains of Wallet and Dart,
Who, in their last race made a capital start.

But their owners lamented that they never got through it.
Alas! They were drowned
In the Thorton Conduit.

Wallet and Dart were two sheepdogs who drowned in one of the goits feeding Thornton Moor Reservoir in 1891. Why they were immortalised in a poorly metered limerick is not recorded.

The Withens' second macabre attribute was its resident ghost. An apocryphal tradition relates that one stormy night in the nineteenth century, a traveller lost his way on the moors and finally collapsed at the hotel's door. The landlord hauled him inside and sat him by the fire, but it was too late and the poor man died of exposure in a chair beside the hearth. His spirit supposedly lingered at Withens and many claimed the fireside seat was always cooler than the surrounding bar.

# 3

# SHIBDEN DALE

## High Sunderland Hall, Horley Green

During its lifetime, High Sunderland was surely the most remarkable building in the region: a castellated gritstone edifice, its exterior festooned with Latinate inscriptions and grotesque statuary. It stood near Horley Green, on the ridge of the hillside overlooking Shibden Dale and could be seen from miles around. Sadly, subsidence caused by mining operations beneath Pepper Hill led to its demolition in 1951; nothing remains but the name of High Sunderland Lane and some examples of the ornamental stonework (currently on display at Shibden Hall).

It is not surprising that High Sunderland – with its Gothic frontage and turbulent history – was swathed in romantic legend. When R. Thurston Hopkins visited the hall in 1949, he reported:

There is a story anyone sleeping in a certain room at High Sunderland would hear footsteps coming down the corridor. A hand would fumble at the door handle and try to open the door. If the hand found the door locked all would be still for a few seconds and

*The exterior of High Sunderland shortly before it was demolished. (Louis Ambler)*

A doorway and attendant grotesque at High Sunderland. (Louis Ambler)

'My fingers closed on the fingers of a little, ice-cold hand! The intense horror of nightmare came over me. I tried to draw back my arm, but the hand clung to it, and a most melancholy voice sobbed "Let me in – let me in!"'

R. Thurston Hopkins suggests that not only did the exterior of High Sunderland suggest itself to Emily Brontë as the model for *Wuthering Heights*, its legend also provided inspiration for Lockwood's dream. Indeed, the whole introductory section of the novel may have first occurred to Emily whilst she was employed at Law Hill nearby.

Although this is a pleasing conceit, it may be too good to be true. High Sunderland was first identified with *Wuthering Heights* by William Sharp in 1904 and later fleshed out by the Halifax historian, T. W. Hanson, in 1924. Meanwhile, Hopkins did not visit High Sunderland to hear the legend until 1949. It is therefore possible that sometime between Sharp's or Hanson's thoughts being published and Hopkins' visit, the tenants of High Sunderland borrowed the legend from the novel to augment the verisimilitude. Nor can we overlook the role of Hopkins: an author who has been accused of embellishing his material.

Nonetheless, the High Sunderland legend differs sufficiently from the dream sequence in *Wuthering Heights* for us to remain open-minded on the issue. The vague narrative certainly has the hallmarks of many late eighteenth- or early nineteenth-century traditions. However, whether Emily Brontë heard this tale about High Sunderland and decided to incorporate it into the text of her novel remains a controversial – but nonetheless pleasing – speculation.

then a hand would tap at the window – just a white hand not forming part of a body … and then would follow bursts of horrible laughter.

Hopkins relates that locals imagined the spectral hand once belonged to a 'most estimable and virtuous lady'. However, her jealous husband grew suspicious and accused the woman of infidelity. She was blameless, but in a fit of passion, he severed her hand with his sword.

This motif of the ghostly hand also seems to correspond with a passage in Emily Brontë's famous novel, *Wuthering Heights*. In Chapter 3, snow forces Mr Lockwood to spend the night at Wuthering Heights, whereupon he experiences a terrifying dream. Annoyed by what he believes to be a tree tapping at the window pane in the wind, Lockwood opens the window in an attempt to catch the offending branches:

## Scout Hall, Shibden

The cadaverous edifice of Scout Hall rears up from Shibden's lesser-frequented upper reaches like the fabled House of Usher. It has been decaying for many decades now, every inch the archetypal haunted house. As long ago as 1959, the architectural historian, Nikolaus Pevsner, described it as 'a half-derelict palace in the deserted English countryside'. Numerous attempts to restore the hall to its former glory have since foundered on this monumental folly and despite its Grade II★ listing, it languishes on English Heritage's Register of Buildings at Risk.

Built around 1680, Scout Hall is an architecturally curious fusion of vernacular and classical influences. The three-storey building supposedly has fifty-two doors, twelve bays and 365 panes of glass – making it a 'calendar house' – whilst a number of fine bas-reliefs depicting hunting scenes decorate the exterior.

The hall was built for John Mitchell, the scion of a prosperous family of yeoman-clothiers who was orphaned and attained his inheritance aged 13. The boy used his new resources to fund a life of indulgence and his guardians did little to curb his adolescent excess.

Mitchell's behaviour scandalised the neighbourhood and the diaries of many of his worthier contemporaries are full of outrage at his antics. Revd Oliver Heywood of Northowram was especially horrified by the house-warming held upon the completion of Scout Hall:

> John Mitchell of Scout, the last week in Christmas to season his new home kept open house, entertained all comers, had fearful ranting work, drinking healths freely; had forty-three dishes at one. I have scarce heard the like in our parts; his wife was the musician. Lord put a stop.

On 8 May 1681, Mitchell staged a horse race on the hilltop between Shibden and

*Scout Hall in the upper Shibden Valley.*

Boothtown – an area known as Swales Moor or Pule Nick, where there is an artificial ski slope today. The event lasted several days and attracted several hundred spectators from across the district, a handful of whom were mowed down by the galloping horses. Mitchell's taste for gambling later brought him trouble though and in 1686 he transferred ownership of Scout Hall to his wife, Mary, to secure it from repossession for his debts.

Mitchell died on 9 May 1696, aged only 37, possibly from injuries sustained in a fall from his horse as he rode furiously down the steep bank above Scout Hall. However, a persistent legend claims he died following a primitive aviation experiment, possibly a balloon, but more often said to be a mechanical device which he launched from a nearby hillside before plummeting to his death when the wings failed.

When the ghost researcher, R. Thurston Hopkins, visited Scout Hall in 1949 – accompanied by the editor of the *Halifax Evening Courier* – he noted a local tradition, 'that John Mitchell still flies his "Scout" flying-machine and that ghostly crashes heard on the hillside resemble the noise made by some heavy contraption falling from a great height on the rocks'. Possibly Shibden folk once told this story, but whether they ever genuinely believed it seems unlikely; especially as the valley so often resounds with quarry blasts and other industrial thrum.

Perhaps less sensationally, Hopkins added that 'several tenants have left after seeing strange shapes drifting about the room and hearing uncanny noises'. As the last tenants at Scout Hall left not too many years after Hopkins' visit this seems credible – although it raises the old conundrum: is the house derelict because it was haunted or do people think it must be haunted because it's derelict? Either way, many children and urban explorers who have investigated the derelict interior of Scout Hall over the years have been disturbed by its uncanny atmosphere and made a hasty exit.

## Coley, Hipperholme

The hamlet of Coley – situated between Hipperholme and Shelf – conjures an atmosphere of otherworldliness like few other settlements in the district. This quality may have been recognised for centuries and there is a persistent tradition that it was once a sacred place; an identification supported by the name of the neighbouring hamlet – Priestley Green – and the abundance of holy wells in the vicinity: St John's Well, Lister Well and Halliwell Syke.

Coley was closely associated with the English Civil Wars in the local psyche – indeed local folklore claims the front of Coley Hall needed to be rebuilt after it had been bombarded by Roundhead cannons (although this may simply have been a confused recollection of extensive renovation work undertaken in 1681).

Speaking to a local newspaper in 1961, a solicitor named Mr Gudgin recalled that his late client, John Herbert Fletcher, had once encountered two Cavaliers at Coley – they were casually stood in the morning room as he entered for breakfast and vanished the moment he tried to speak to them. A guest of Mr Fletcher also witnessed the apparition on one occasion; it manifested in an old chair 'wearing long black riding boots and old fashioned clothes; he wore his red hair long and curly, and smoked a very long clay pipe'.

*An apotropaic head guarding the gateway to Coley Hall.*

The newspaper was subsequently contacted by one Mr Watkinson, whose childhood was spent at Coley. He recalled a legend that a Royalist soldier had been caught hiding in a priest hole and slain. He was shown the supposed priest hole by his aunt, who told him that the discolouration on the floorboards was the soldier's bloodstain, which would never wash off no matter how hard it was scrubbed. Many will recognise this as a common motif in English ghost lore, also attached to buildings such as Calverly Hall and Oakwell Hall in West Yorkshire.

The phantom Cavalier was witnessed again by Mrs Pickles in the 1960s. There was only one apparition on this occasion, reclined insouciantly against a mantelpiece, and once again he disappeared as soon as Mrs Pickles confronted him.

Mr Gudgin – the solicitor – also mentioned a spectral 'white lady' called Caroline Anne. Guests had woken up in the middle of the night to find the bed violently shaking and another visitor's sleep had been disturbed by a sensation like cobwebs being draped across her body.

Such poltergeist activity was not unusual: phantom bells often rang and

Mrs Pickles' dog would frequently bridle at invisible presences. She also recalled the experience of a mechanic who'd been working on a car when he was showered by soil from an unknown source. As he checked for the culprit, a sod of mud containing a large stone struck the component he'd been working on, undoing all his labour. The mechanic was so furious he checked thoroughly for the perpetrator but there nowhere for anybody to hide.

In more recent years, motorists have reported seeing a grubby Royalist soldier on horseback riding along the lane around Coley. The witnesses investigated the possibility of a local fair or re-enactment, but they could find nothing that might account for the anachronistic attire of this horseman. A sighting occurred in 1998, suggesting that the ghosts of Coley are active still and may haunt that sequestered spot for many generations to come.

## Sowood House, Coley

Located at the junction of Halifax and Coley Road, Sowood House was constructed in 1631 by the prosperous Whitley family of Northowram. Like many residents in the vicinity of Coley at that time – including the tenants of Wynteredge and Coley Hall – the Whitley family were staunch Royalists; possibly even clandestine Catholic recusants. For some reason, John Whitley and wife Grace did not tarry at Sowood House and only seven years later they built themselves a new home at Norwood Green called Rookes Hall.

Little else is known about the Whitleys or even the many subsequent

*Sowood House at Coley.*

tenants of Sowood House and as such it is difficult to say exactly who concealed a human skull in the fabric of the building. It was discovered during renovations to the house in 1968, contained in a lead box hidden behind brickwork in the chimney.

Frank Drury, who was restoring the property, immediately notified the police of the discovery who sent the skull for forensic examination at the University of Leeds. They were satisfied that the skull was not evidence of a recent murder and passed it to the archaeology department, who established that the relic had probably been concealed in the chimney when the house was built in the early seventeenth century. More puzzling, however, was an inscription on the bone itself; sadly this was no longer very legible and could not be deciphered.

Although the archaeologists were stumped, a letter sent by an 80-year-old resident of Southowram to a local newspaper, following its coverage of the skull's discovery, is rather more instructive. She recalled:

I remember my mother telling me about the skull over seventy years ago.

She said the skull was found in an iron box in the chimney breast. It was taken to Coley and buried in the churchyard.

Afterwards the house began to be haunted by cries of, 'Where is my head?!' When, on the advice of the vicar, it was replaced in the chimney the cries ceased. My great-grandfather was a churchwarden of St John's, Coley and was present when the skull was put back.

The skull may also be connected with a legend concerning a headless apparition that haunts the churchyard at St John's.

This places the skull in a unique category of relics known as 'guardian skulls' or, more luridly, 'screaming skulls' in reference to the supernatural disturbances that follow their removal from a house. The seventeenth century was an epoch in which such folk magic flourished and numerous objects have been discovered in the fabric of building from that period including: witch bottles, horse skulls, old shoes and even mummified cats. The latter were particularly common in Calderdale and have been discovered at Slead Hall in Brighouse and the church of St Thomas à Beckett at Heptonstall.

Such artefacts are often found walled up at 'liminal' threshold locations in the building; these include roof-spaces, gables, windows, doorways and chimneys – places were malign spiritual forces might gain access to the house. Similarly, guardian skulls protect the house from baleful influences and ensure the prosperity of its inhabitants – as long as the skull is treated with respect. If it is slighted in any way, or removed from the house, misfortune and paranormal activity invariably persist until the skull is returned to its rightful position in the house.

There are only a handful of other places in Britain with a guardian skull legend attached: Calgarth Hall in Cumbria, Burton Agnes Hall in East Yorkshire, Tunstead Farm in Derbyshire and Wardley Hall in Lancashire to name but a few. The Sowood House skull lacks the developed legend of these other sites and whatever origin story was attached to it has now been lost: we do not know to whom it belonged or why that particular individual's skull was considered worth preserving.

*Church of St John the Baptist at Coley.*

The political affiliation of the Whitley family during the English Civil Wars may be relevant in this respect, as guardian skulls are often associated with Royalist luminaries or Catholic martyrs. For instance, the skull at Wardley Hall in Lancashire is thought to belong to St Ambrose Barlow – a Benedictine monk who was hung, drawn and quartered in 1641 for offering Mass to recusant families across the county.

The archaeologists who examined the skull at the University of Leeds thought the lettering etched on the bone may have record its identity. However, it seems equally likely that this was some magical incantation intended to ensure the talisman's potency.

They also speculated that it might have belonged to a criminal executed by the Halifax Gibbet. Although this seems improbable, it is not impossible: the majority of victims of the gibbet were petty thieves and if a human skull was considered puissant in its own right (much like the hand of an executed criminal) then it does not seem to have been difficult to procure one.

## Walterclough Hall, Walterclough

The picturesque Walterclough Valley is technically the lower reach of Shibden Dale as it runs from Hipperholme towards Slead Syke and Brighouse. During this tract, Shibden Brook becomes known as the Red Beck due to the high content of iron oxide in the surrounding soil, which stains the water a vivid rusty colour. During the nineteenth and early twentieth century, it was famous as the location of Sunny Vale

Pleasure Gardens, which once enjoyed a reputation comparable to somewhere like Alton Towers today.

On the hillside above Sunny Vale there used to be a gaunt ruin known as Walterclough Hall. It had been sliding into dereliction since at least 1919 and a bomb dropped nearby during the Second World War later expedited the transition. Eventually only the façade of the east wing and the rooms immediately behind remained standing, whilst a working farm had grown up around its shell.

One fine summer day in the late 1960s, a gentleman we shall call Stuart – who'd worked on Walterclough Farm in his youth – decided to explore the ruins of the hall, accompanied by his wife, Jean, and her mother, Dorothy. As they reached the top of the rotten, creaking stairs, the older woman stopped abruptly; gripped her son-in-law's arm and stifled a scream. Although neither Stuart nor Jean could see anything, Dorothy's reaction had unnerved them and they evacuated the building as quickly as they possibly could.

Back in the sunshine, an ashen Dorothy explained that through one of the shattered window panes she'd seen a man she knew to be dead standing by a farm gate, beckoning her forward. Yet the wide open fields all around were now empty; the figure could not have crossed them without being seen. He had simply vanished.

The three sat for a while to allow Dorothy to recover, then proceeded to cross the farmyard towards the lane and continue their walk. As they passed alongside a barn, a shower of stones hit the wall with phenomenal violence, barely missing the family. Once again,

nobody could be seen for miles around (although there are thick hedges in that area today, at the time there was nowhere to hide amongst the open fields or along the lane). The incident left the explorers further convinced that some presence was determined they leave that place with haste.

Considering the history of the hall, the fury exhibited in that invitation to depart Walterclough is not surprising. The homestead after which the valley was named is first recorded in 1379 and it was owned by the Hemmingway family for many centuries. However, the story of the site really begins in 1654 when the Walker family bought the estate and built a new hall in the manorial-vernacular style of that period.

Like many wealthy Calderdale dynasties, the Walker family made their fortune in the wool trade and by the mid-eighteenth century it was a substantial enterprise. John Walker Sr was a generous man and at some point he adopted his orphaned nephew, Jack Sharp, who he raised as his own and groomed to take on a role in the family business. When John Walker Sr retired in the 1760s, his eldest son – Richard Walker – displayed no interest in the business or the estate, so the old man placed Sharp in charge of the entirety – including the trade and all its assets, plus the Walterclough estate with all its fixtures and fittings.

When John Walker Sr retired to York, he left Jack Sharp with the run of things. The nephew had grown arrogant with his preferment; he soon alienated his cousins with his boorishness and poor temper, until finally they left him alone at Walterclough Hall. But although the Walker children had little interest in the business or estate, Sharp was no more faithful to it and rapidly squandered its resources on gambling and drink.

In 1771, John Walker Sr died and although the laws of primogeniture ensured that his estate passed to his eldest son, by that time the Walker family had lost all influence over Walterclough. Jack Sharp was only evicted following much legal wrangling and that cuckoo in their nest had his revenge before he left.

When the younger son – John Walker Jr – took up residency with his new wife at Walterclough, they discovered that Sharp had run amok. He'd wrecked the fabric and vandalised the fixtures to the extent that only two rooms were still habitable, then stolen all the heirlooms, furniture, plate, silverware and linen.

Worse was to come. In 1778, Sharp built himself a new house at Law Hill in Southowram – conspicuously over-looking Walterclough. He purposefully chose this location for its proximity to his former family, so that he might constantly remind them of his existence. Sharp then proceeded systematically to corrupt John Walker Jr's cousin, Sam Stead, initiating the boy in all his own manifold iniquities.

Eventually, Stead was ruined and forced to turn to his cousin John for charity. The family gave him shelter at Walterclough Hall, where he repaid their generosity by teaching the children oaths and defiance, whilst generally making a nuisance of himself. Nonetheless, the family were probably relieved, as Jack Sharp had also succumbed to bankruptcy and sold Law Hill House in 1799. His fate thereafter is unknown.

If this story sounds familiar, it is because many commentators have observed its parallels with *Wuthering Heights*. In that tale, Mr Earnshaw adopts a foundling called Heathcliff, who grows up to become an arrogant and

*Law Hill House, Southowram.*

ill-tempered debauchee. He proceeds to gain mastery over the Earnshaw's eponymous home, thereby revenging himself on his foster brother, Hindley, for slights against him during their childhood. Then, still unsatisfied, he lures Hindley's son, Hareton, into dissipation and vice.

These correspondence between the story of Walterclough Hall and *Wuthering Heights* are more than just a coincidence. In 1825, some decades after Jack Sharp had left Law Hill House, it became Miss Patchett's Ladies' Academy and for several months in 1837–38, a 19-year-old Emily Brontë worked there as a governess.

Emily's time at Law Hill was not a happy one. In addition to homesickness, her sister Charlotte recalled that she endured 'hard labour from 6 in the morning until near 11 at night, with only one half-hour of exercise in between' and upon leaving, told the pupils that she 'preferred the dog to any of them'. Nonetheless, Emily will have heard the story of Walterclough Hall, Jack Sharp and Law Hill's construction; the inspiration it provided for her masterpiece is clear.

Unsurprisingly – as the scene of such misery for the girl – the ghost of Emily Brontë has often been attached to Law Hill House. The Marshall family, who lived there until the 1980s, believed her apparition haunted the third-storey of the building; at 12.30 p.m. every Sunday the family heard chairs and tables being moved around the room overhead, even though the room was unoccupied. One resident even saw a shadowy figure looking out of a window on the upper floor.

They also reported typical poltergeist activity, such as doors forcefully opening by themselves and dogs reacting to some invisible presence. Of course, there is no reason that the spectre should belong to Emily Brontë – the Marshalls made this assumption – but, even if we accept the existence of ghosts according to traditional schemata, it could just as easily be the spirit of that old blackguard, Jack Sharp, attempting to drive yet another family from their home as he had driven them from Walterclough.

## Coldwell Hill, Southowram

Prior to his death in 1823, Jonathan Walsh of Coldwell Hill between Southowram and Shibden, was the terror of Halifax parish. A wealthy gentleman-farmer, woollen-manufacturer and rentier, Walsh invested his prodigious income in two directions: moneylending and endless litigation against his neighbours and those he perceived to have wronged him. Such individuals were numerous and one of his long-suffering contemporaries claimed Walsh would 'rather spend a pound for law than a penny for ale'.

Even the mild-mannered Caroline Walker of Walterclough Hall denounced Walsh as an 'old usurer' who was 'a torment to himself and everyone else'. The man rode around the district on a mule and used his riding crop to whip anybody who antagonised him. He was particularly contemptuous towards the clergy, and local ministers were often the target of his ranting ire. Revd Henry Colthurst, the Vicar of Halifax in 1790, found Walsh so boorish and tiresome that he allegedly hid if he saw Walsh coming.

This anti-clerical – perhaps even atheistic – iconoclasm may have been the reason he refused burial in consecrated ground and instead chose to be interred

*Shibden Hall Lane near Coldwell Hill.*

on his own land. Walsh finally died on 11 February 1823 at the grand old age of 82. Unfortunately for his beneficiaries, he expired at a house on Horton Street in Halifax rather than his farm at Coldwell Hill; he was not a small man – the coffin measured more than 6ft – and his pallbearers were obliged to carry it from the town centre up the steep flank of Beacon Hill to the field in which he'd chosen to be buried.

Moreover, as Walsh had stipulated that he was to be buried at midnight by candlelight, they were compelled to carry it there in darkness on a wintry night. His wife had already been buried in one corner of the chosen field; her grave was marked by a cairn, and Walsh left instructions that he should be buried in a stone vault at the opposite point.

He also specified that he should be laid with his feet facing west and his head facing east – the opposite direction to that dictated by religion convention. However, Walsh was not concerned that his ghost might walk after his death and in fact had chosen to be inhumed in unhallowed ground with precisely such an afterlife in mind; he'd been so plagued by travellers on the old road between

Halifax and Leeds trespassing on his land, that he had chosen to be buried in a field adjacent to the highway so that he might haunt them for evermore.

Unfortunately for Walsh, the local folk he so despised had the last laugh. Following his death, his heirs sold the land on which the couple were buried to the Listers of Shibden Hall who later leased it to Maude & Dyson – a quarrying outfit which sought to exploit the area for stone.

Thus, in 1896 – seventy-three years after Jonathan Walsh had been buried – his corpse was exhumed. Much like Walsh himself, Maude & Dyson evidently had little notion of conventional piety: rather than rebury his remains, they placed them on display and charged the public 2*d* each to inspect them. Over the following week several thousand people with an appetite for sensation came to see the macabre exhibit – until it prematurely concluded when the skeleton was 'kicked to pieces by drunkards'.

Nonetheless, local folk still believed that Pump Lane, Wakefield Gate and Halifax Old Road (also known as Shibden Hall Lane) were haunted in the vicinity of Coldwell Hill. A reference to the belief by local historian T. W. Hanson in 1924 suggests the superstition still persisted at that time.

Curiously, a local man recently reported a ghostly experience in the winter of 1979–80 on Shibden Hall Lane very close to Coldwell Hill. He recalls:

As I was a short distance from the houses near the railway viaduct, I saw a tall, thin figure of a man – all in black with a pointed hat – emerge through closed gates and start walking towards Hipperholme. The figure seemed to

*Shibden Hall.*

keep a steady pace ahead of me and then suddenly disappeared. On reaching the spot where I had seen the figure emerge I could see no footprints, nor were there any footprints on my continued journey to Hipperholme.

## Shibden Hall, Shibden

Shibden Hall is one of the most striking domestic residences in Calderdale and one of the oldest – the original timber-framed house was erected in 1420 and then cased in stone in 1504. It provided inspiration for Emily Brontë who may have partly based Thrushcross Grange in *Wuthering Heights* on Shibden Hall. Although it has been embellished over the years, much of the original building survives; its historical importance led to the hall being donated to the Halifax Corporation in 1931, who converted it

into a folk museum the following year. It is so well preserved that it has become a popular shooting location for period dramas featuring a Tudor manor house.

Unusually, supernatural activity has only been encountered recently at Shibden Hall. Tony Sharpe, who'd worked as an attendant at the hall for twenty-six years, told the BBC in 2007: 'You see things out of the corner of your eye. I've heard noises, we hear creaks and groans. I've never seen any figures but I've heard voices and I've heard footsteps. We also smell lavender and fresh pipe tobacco as if someone's just lit a pipe.'

Although this may sound like standard fare, he continues: 'The worst thing that happened to me was earlier on this year. I was opening the side gate and it was dark – about half past seven in the morning. I was suddenly aware of this big black shape above the left of my head … It was weird. It wasn't a bird …

[but] like a big black cloak.' Meanwhile, guests have reported being struck on the back of the head by an invisible hand a number of times, so forcefully that other people nearby noticed the impact.

A 'grey lady' is also sometimes seen at Shibden Hall and although Tony Sharpe dismissed this as 'just folklore', a number of tourists claim to have seen the apparition. One visitor remembers exploring the hall as a child during the 1960s and witnessing a spectral woman 'in a long sweeping dress' pass through the wall of a room near the top of the stairs. Her report is corroborated by staff at Shibden Hall, to whom people have reported similar experiences on a number of occasions over the years.

This 'grey lady' is often identified with tragic Ann Walker, whose story is intertwined with the hall's history. In 1614, the hall was bought by the Lister family, who occupied it for successive generations until 1931. The most interesting member of this clan was Anne Lister, who inherited the hall in 1826, aged 38. Anne made numerous improvements during her residency; she commissioned the Gothic tower on the west gable to house her library and laid out Shibden Park, which has since provided recreation for generations of Calderdale folk.

Miss Lister was a formidable individual; well educated, well invested and well travelled. She journeyed through much of Europe and Anatolia, during which adventures she became the first person to conquer Vignemale and the first woman to ascent Mount Perdu – both summits in the Pyrenees. Meanwhile, back at home in Halifax, Lister was a canny businesswoman; in addition to the rents she received from her Shibden estate, she invested in mining operations through the district and funded the Godley Cutting, allowing the new Leeds–Halifax Turnpike to cross Beacon Hill.

Lister's business acumen created a number of rivals who were keen to discredit her, especially those who did not believe mining or quarrying to be a suitable enterprise for a woman! Much malicious gossip was spread through the local press, whilst her supposedly 'masculine' features and dress earned her the spiteful nickname 'Gentleman Jack'. Sometimes her life was even threatened; on one occasion a local mob gathered near Shibden Hall at night and were heard to fire a few pistol shots in her direction.

Today Lister is most famous for her diaries, which she kept from 1806 until her death in 1840, over twenty-seven volumes and approximately 4 million words. An estimated one-sixth of this total was written in code, which was not deciphered until 1988. They were written thus because they detailed her relationship and sexual encounters with other women; a profoundly scandalous confession during that era. Lister's liberated status and her candidness in print has led her to be dubbed 'the first modern lesbian'.

Lister enjoyed a succession of relationships with other woman over the course of her life; indeed, her sexuality revealed itself at an early age and she was expelled from Mr Lumley's Boarding School for Ladies aged 12. However, her most significant union was with Ann Walker, the heiress to Cliffe Hill at Lightcliffe, whom she met in 1834. Their union was even consecrated by an 'unofficial' marriage ceremony at Holy Trinity church in York. When Lister died on 22 September 1840 – from an infection caught whilst travelling in the Caucasus – she left her entire estate to Walker.

Sadly, Walker had always suffered from mental health problems and her condition only deteriorated following her lover's death. As a result, she only spent three years at Shibden before she was certified as being of unfit mind and confined to an asylum near York. It is said that prior to her removal from the hall, Walker had barricaded herself in a bedchamber called the 'red room' where she attempted suicide. When a constable broke down the door, he found her bleeding profusely, surrounded by rotting uneaten food.

Shibden Hall passed back to the Lister family following Ann Walker's eviction, whilst the unfortunate woman died naturally at Cliffe Hill in 1854. Nonetheless, some believe her unhappy presence has lingered around the 'red room' and sightings of the 'grey lady' have only added to their conviction.

# 4

# THE LOWER CALDER VALLEY

## Church Lane, Brighouse

A nondescript terrace on a town centre byway, Church Lane may seem like an incongruous location for one of Brighouse's most alarming hauntings, but it was once the scene of extensive and unnerving poltergeist activity. Over the course of 1985, the homeowners, Jack and Brenda Mansley, and especially their 25-year-old daughter Karen, were terrorised by a range of aural, kinetic and atmospheric phenomena. The similarities to the occurrences at Thornhill Road in Rastrick are numerous; but while that episode has been referenced in several regional surveys of contemporary ghost lore, the Church Lane poltergeist has been largely overlooked.

Karen first suspected that something was amiss when she arrived home one day to discover her jewellery box wrenched open and its contents strewn across the room. However, this was only the beginning. She would return home to discover all the lights in the house on, coats strewn across the floor and all the taps running until the sink was ready to overflow. Other members of the family – including ones who didn't

live there – witnessed these disturbances too. At such times, people said the house was icily cold even though the fire was blazing.

Soon the phenomena grew even more conspicuous and threatening. Karen found her birth certificate torn up in the corner of a room, a cherished book stuffed with rubbish in the bin, and a full-length mirror thrown from the wall onto her bed. Meanwhile, doors, cupboards and drawers began to open and slam shut of their own accord, floorboards creaked as if somebody was walking heavily across them, and mysterious crashes resounded from under the bedroom floor. By this point, Karen was too terrified to remain

Church Lane, Brighouse.

in the house alone and was sleeping with the light on.

By the end of 1985, the Mansley family were at their wits' end and called in a Spiritualist medium to resolve the haunting. Initially he suspected the presence was the spirit of a little girl – possibly Mary Manley, whose father James built and lived in these houses at the junction of Commercial Street with Church Lane. She'd died in 1843 at the tender age of 7 and was buried in St Martin's churchyard nearby. However, as the manifestations grew more savage, the medium began to suspect a male presence, possibly a violent alcoholic searching the house for valuables to pawn.

Sadly for the Mansley family, their Spiritualist saviour did not seem particularly confident of his efforts to persuade the spirit to move on. After visiting the house, he told the family that matters would 'build to a crescendo' but sadly the local press lost interest at this point and the conclusion of the case has not been recorded.

Many paranormal researchers dismiss the idea that poltergeists are the restless spirits of the dead, and instead believe them to be a form of undirected, negative psychic energy generated by tensions amongst the occupants of the house themselves. Certainly, reading between the lines of the newspaper reports from the time, you get the impression it was a febrile environment in the house and so perhaps the poltergeist doubtless left when Karen did or perhaps even when the familial dynamic altered for the better. If so, the Spiritualist medium was right to doubt his ability to achieve any positive result.

# Clifton Woods & Coal Pit Lane, Clifton

Sometime between 9 p.m. on New Year's Eve 1832 and 3 p.m. the following afternoon, a 20-year-old woman by the name of Elizabeth Rayner was brutally slain in Clifton Woods. The body was discovered by her younger brothers, John and Simeon, amongst the trees only 200 yards or so from her home in Well Lane. An inquest held at the nearby Black Horse Inn several days later determined that her throat had been cut by a left-handed assailant. They also found that Elizabeth, an unmarried woman who lived with her parents, had been pregnant when she died.

Tragically, Elizabeth Rayner's murderer was never brought to justice – although it has been implied that many residents of the close-knit village of Clifton had their suspicions about the perpetrator's identity. A second inquest was held and Sir George Armytage of nearby Kirklees Hall, a wealthy local landowner and justice of the peace, offered a reward of £200 to anybody offering information which would lead to the killer's arrest. These efforts proved in vain.

Violent death in a small community always leaves a psychic scar and it not surprising that Clifton folk still recalled the murder of Elizabeth Rayner long after her death. Even as late as the mid-twentieth century, local children were warned not to play in Clifton Woods because 'a murder once happened there'.

In later life, Elizabeth's brother John 'Jack' Rayner ran a sweet shop from a cottage on Towngate. He often used to regale his young customers with the story of the murder. He would tell them how he vividly recalled hearing a

*Clifton Woods by Coal Pit Lane.*

'soughing noise like the squeal of a hare in distress' at the time when the killing must have occurred and doubtless such Grand Guignol repetitions kept the memory of his sister's unavenged murder alive in the local folk memory.

The stretch of Coal Pit Lane, which bordered Clifton Woods close to where the body was found, was long regarded with anxiety by local folk, many of whom lacked the courage to pass that way after dark. The spot was considered to be haunted by the unquiet spirit of the murdered girl and villagers also claimed that a strange sound like the 'squeal of a hare in distress' was often heard and regarded with some dread.

Even more curious is an apparition which has been encountered by at least five descendants of Elizabeth Rayner's brother, John. It was last seen by a member of the family at a house in Bradford Road during the mid-1980s, who described this ancestral shade as a tall, cloaked silhouette. Given the attire of the figure and its connection with the family, some of the witnesses have speculated whether it might not be the spectre of their ancestor's murderer, continuing to victimise the Rayner lineage even in death.

## The Globe Inn, Rastrick

The history of The Globe inn at Rastrick is regrettably obscure due to the loss of all of its records in a fire at the brewery by which it was once owned. It seems to have been converted into a pub from three separate dwelling houses sometime in the late eighteenth or nineteenth century; and its position on Rastrick Common – formerly a stretch of the

The Globe inn, Rastrick.

principle highway between Wakefield and Elland – suggests that it was originally a coaching inn.

In 1982, Geoff Clayton, the new landlord at The Globe, reported a range of typical poltergeist phenomena at the pub. Glasses leapt from their shelves; pictures were reluctant to stay on the walls; dogs refused to enter the bottle-store and often growled in its general direction.

This was all predictable fare for a pub ghost. However, it was accompanied by a persistent tradition that a former landlord had committed suicide in the bottle-store sometime in the nineteenth century. The unfortunate landlord's name was Old Harry and his ghost was believed to haunt the pub by bar staff and regular customers alike.

The association between suicide and haunting is a relic of medieval eschatology. Early Christian theologians considered suicide an act of 'self-murder'; a mortal sin which it was impossible to repent. As such, suicides were denied burial in consecrated ground and forced to wander the earth as they could not gain access to the precincts of Heaven. Wherever a suicide had occurred, rumours of a haunting swiftly followed. The converse is also true – where spectral activity is experienced, people assume an unhallowed death such as suicide must have taken place.

Curiously, in the case of The Globe, this tradition proved to be well founded. Following coverage of the haunting in the local press, an 83-year-old gentleman named Fred Marshall contacted the pub's landlord to corroborate the rumour of suicide. Mr Marshall, who now lived at Sheepridge, had spent his childhood at The Globe where his father was once the landlord and he knew the story of the tragedy well.

On 17 May 1910, Fred's father, Albert Marshall, hanged himself in the bottle-store. His son had only been 11 at the time, but evidently bore his father no malice: he even seemed quite pleased to know that his father's spirit might be at large in Rastrick still. Meanwhile, the case supports the folklorist's conviction that although local tradition may sometimes grow confused, it is still capable of accurately preserving the memory of certain events down through the generations.

## Thornhill Road, Rastrick

A seventeenth-century cottage nestles incongruously amidst Victorian terraces on the road between Brighouse and Rastrick. It was built around 1690, possibly a lodging house for travellers in the days when packhorse routes often took them through the village. In the 1970s it was converted into two separate dwellings and shortly thereafter became the home of Peter and Marilyn Auty, who experienced one of the most extensive and widely reported hauntings in the district over the following decade.

The case was first brought to the attention of the public by the author and ghost hunter Terence Whitaker, but it was subsequently documented by the local press and has since featured in a number of regional paranormal guides. Whitaker first published his account in 1983, but the Autys had experienced an array of phenomena since they'd moved in several years earlier.

Although they claimed the ghost was not a poltergeist because it lacked a kinetic aspect it still met many of the criteria for a 'noisy spirit': disturbances included a high-pitched whistling which could be heard over the noise of the television; thudding from the ceiling as if somebody was stamping across the room above; a persistent rapping as if somebody was tapping glass with a coin; and perhaps most curiously, the sound of an ornamental bell the family kept on a landing at the top of the stairs – despite the fact its clapper had been removed.

Marilyn Auty was especially persecuted by the presence. She once heard somebody urgently whispering her name, as if they were in distress, and thought it was her husband – who was working in the garden – but he denied calling her. On another occasion, she had gone to bed alone one night and was disturbed by the sound of heavy breathing which lasted for five to ten minutes and left her cowering beneath the bedclothes, so perturbed that she no longer felt comfortable in the house on her own.

Although the activity was primarily auditory, the couple also encountered visible phenomena from time to time. Marilyn Auty twice witnessed an apparition that resembled 'filmy-like smoke'; once in the hallway when she was sat alone in the living-room and again when

*Thornhill Road, Rastrick.*

she was using the vacuum cleaner on the staircase. When Terence Whitaker attempted to photograph the point at which this amorphous form manifested, his camera repeatedly failed but functioned perfectly when he left the house.

Peter Auty also saw what he described as a figure wearing a grey cowl, greatly resembling a monk, pass through the living room and disappear through the wall next to an internal door. The figure appeared to be cut off at the knees and the Auty family later discovered that the floor of the room had originally been lower prior to renovation. This encounter resembles Harry Martindale's famous encounter with a spectral Roman legion in the cellar of the Treasurer's House at York in 1953.

Such sightings have supported the hypothesis that ghosts are not the spirits of the dead but a form of automated playback recorded on an environmental medium such as the fabric of a building. They are not sentient entities but mindlessly repeat the same motions over and over according to the original layout of their haunt; an interpretation known as 'residual haunting' or 'Stone Tape theory' – after a supernatural drama broadcast by the BBC in 1972. It is a popular naturalistic theory of ghosts, but in this case it doesn't seem to fit the other phenomena experienced at Thornhill Road.

There is evidence that the haunting has endured and in 2011, the latest resident of the property next door (but originally part of the same building) was plagued by mysterious phenomena similar to that experienced by the Autys. This included the sound of the broken bell and a noise like running footsteps along the upstairs landing.

She also witnessed an apparition which she described as having 'very dark features and longish but mangy patchy stubble and very tired puffy eyes … He had no hat on but a dark thick collar'. The figure looked straight at the tenant, who found the experience so overwhelming that she started to sob uncontrollably. Perhaps significantly, the tenant had no previous knowledge of the building's haunted history.

## Boggart House, Southowram

The word 'boggart' was once a common dialect term used throughout the West Riding of Yorkshire and East Lancashire to denote a mischievous or even malevolent supernatural presence. Prior to the rise of the Gothic and Spiritualist traditions in the late eighteenth and nineteenth century, taxonomies of the Otherworld were less strictly defined than they are today: hence boggart might have been used to refer to anything from a hilltop hobgoblin to a household faerie, from a headless apparition to a prototypical poltergeist.

A 'boggart house' was any house reputed to be vexatiously haunted, or in some other way uncanny – for instance, there was formerly a boggart house at Pellon which local folklore claims belonged to a man who worked the Halifax Gibbet. It was also commonly attached to derelict buildings. Over the generations the 'boggart house' toponym has been attached to old dwellings in Brierley, Midgley, Seacroft, Esholt and more; in some cases, the name stuck – even after the details of the supposed haunting were forgotten – and so its reputation endured into the twentieth century.

Boggart House in Southowram stands alone in Binns Wood, overlooking the valley of Cromwell Bottom (once known to locals as the 'faery glen' due to its tranquil character). It was probably built during the early nineteenth century to serve as a gatehouse to the estate of the manorial Ashday Hall nearby.

However, with the waning fortunes of the landed gentry in the early twentieth century, the gatehouse was abandoned and it first gained notoriety during this period. Many folk who grew up in Southowram between the 1920s and the 1950s vividly recall the derelict house and its ghostly reputation.

In 1961, the property was purchased by Peter Turner and extensively restored. Although the house brimmed with the vitality of human life once more, the family soon discovered they'd acquired the eponymous spirit along with the other chattels.

Speaking to a local newspaper in 1981, Peter Turner reported that he often heard strange rapping noises in the night and witnessed lights turning themselves on. Perhaps more startlingly, a visiting relative encountered the apparition of a short man with a ginger beard in a cupboard under the stairs – a visage very

*Boggart House at Ashday near Southowram.*

much like the traditional depiction of the 'household faery' aspect of a boggart's myriad forms.

Thirty years later, Peter Turner's oldest daughter, Susan, lives at Boggart House with her family and confirms that the hauntings are still active. She said, 'There are still plenty of unexplained things going on, like coming home to a freshly boiled kettle of water and lights switching on and off but nothing too nasty.'

Such phenomena is the hallmark of poltergeist activity, reminding us that a boggart is a fundamentally protean entity which not only encompasses a spectrum of supernatural belief but embodies each band with impunity. It is singularly appropriate that 'spectrum' derives from the Latin root for an apparition – which also gave us the word 'spectre'. Such synchronicity reminds us that the supernatural order has always been a continuum and it has always been in flux; as such, the study of this order is poetic rather than systemic.

## Elland Road, Cromwell Bottom

Many residents of Brighouse and Elland will remember a large derelict shell at the side of Elland Road. The house had been abandoned sometime in the mid-twentieth century after it was gutted by fire and its walls were blackened with smoke; most windows were shattered and the roof had caved in, whilst its internal fabric – plasterwork, staircase, floorboards – had long since rotted away. Successive plans to develop it as a hotel, restaurant or nursing home fell through over the years, but it was finally converted into residential apartments in 1994.

During the early 1980s it regularly attracted teenagers bent on exploring the ruins of the 'spooky old house'. One such group even discovered a secret staircase behind some oak-panelling that ran parallel to the main stairs. They did not progress beyond a similar panel at the top of the stairs because the smell of Woodbine cigarettes was so strong that they imagined somebody must have been smoking beyond it and did not wish to be caught by adults or intrude upon other, potentially bigger adolescents.

On another occasion, they managed to find the entrance to the cellar and descended to explore (oddly they found it contained an old boat and stash of fairground equipment). One member of the trio broke off to empty his bladder – only to appear two minutes later in a state of panic, demanding to know which one of them had whispered in his ear whilst he was urinating. No one had and each could account for the other's whereabouts at the time. Seized by the potential implications of this scenario they beat a hasty retreat and never explored the cellar again!

Three decades later, residents of the flats have reported seeing the ghost of a bearded gentleman at the bottom of a narrow stairwell. Only seen by other men, he would nod in acknowledgement as he passed by and then vanish. This part of the building also frequently smelled of Woodbine cigarettes, although the communal areas of building were non-smoking and none of the tenants were known to smoke this rare brand in their flats. Although the exact layout of the house is not clear, it seems probable that the staircase on which these cigarettes have been smelt recently is the same staircase discovered by the teenagers in the 1980s.

The original property was built in 1820 by the Rawson family, who owned many mining and quarrying operations in the vicinity at the time – they gave their surname to the Rawsons' Arms pub, which has now been converted into offices for W. T. Knowles & Son Clay Pipe Work. However, by the mid-nineteenth century, the property had passed to the Edwards family and Geoffrey Otho Charles Edwards was born in the house in 1876. He served as Second Lieutenant in the 3rd Battalion Duke of Wellington's Regiment during the First World War and died on 7 July 1916 – one of many thousands killed at the Battle of the Somme. Unfiltered Woodbines – sometimes known as 'gaspers' – were the most popular brand of cigarette during the First World War and have been associated with soldiers ever since.

## Old Hall, Elland

Elland Old Hall was a thirteenth-century cruck-framed building cased in stone which formerly stood on Exley Lane overlooking Elland Bridge – site of an ancient crossing on the River Calder. The hall was originally built as the seat of the de Eland family, who'd been connected with the town since the early medieval period. Unfortunately it was demolished in 1976 as it obstructed the route of the new Elland bypass (now known as the Calderdale Way).

During the fourteenth century, Old Hall was home to Sir John de Eland, High Sheriff of West Yorkshire and High Steward to the Earls of Warren. In 1341, he murdered Sir Robert Beaumont – a follower of the Warrens' rival, the Earl of Lancaster – at Crosland Hall near Huddersfield. Beaumont's sons were spared and after several years of lying low in Lancashire they enacted their revenge. The Beaumont faction ambushed Sir John de Eland's retinue between Brookfoot and Lane Head as they travelled to preside over the sheriff's tourn at Brighouse in 1353, and many were slain amidst a 'great effusion of blood'.

King Edward III placed a bounty on young Adam Beaumont and his confederates for the massacre, forcing them to retreat to the fastness of the Furness Fells in Lancashire. However, they returned the following year to avenge themselves on the remaining members of the de Eland family, ambushing the junior Sir John de Eland at a ford over the River Calder near Elland Mill, where Elland Bridge stands today. They killed Sir John outright and wounded his infant son, who later died of his injuries at Old Hall.

Several of the murderers were caught, but Adam Beaumont successfully escaped and sought penance fighting in the Holy Land with the Knights of St John of Jerusalem. Meanwhile, Isobel de Eland – Sir John's widow – subsequently remarried Sir John Savile of Elland New Hall, following which the de Eland association with Old Hall came to an end. With such a colourful history, Elland Old Hall was inevitably steeped in folklore; although by the time such traditions were recorded, only the kitchen remained of the original medieval building. Numerous secret subterranean passages were supposed to lead to a variety of destinations – including the church of St Mary, Elland New Hall and Clay House at Greetland.

The tales might have been inspired by a strange cavity in fabric of the west wing. The 'vacancy of considerable size' (approximately 6ftx4ft) ran all the way from the foundations to the roof and it was impossible to access: whatever the original purpose of this 'secret chamber,' it had been hermetically sealed many centuries ago. One of Old Hall's ghosts was suspected to belong to an individual who'd been trapped in this space; or else the ghost itself had been imprisoned in the hollow following an exorcism – the record is not entirely clear.

In the nineteenth century the spectre frequently bothered an old woman who lived in what was once a kitchen, before the hall had been partitioned into three separate residences. The fireplace in this room was alleged to conceal a secret passage and the lady reported that she had seen it open without human agency; as if some ghost was using the tunnels as its thoroughfare. Sadly the identity of Old Hall's spirits was not documented and with at least three scions of the de Eland

*The Fleece Inn, Elland.*

family murdered – two in cold blood – there is no shortage of candidates.

## The Fleece Inn, Elland

The Fleece Inn on Westgate is one of Elland's most venerable establishments. It was built around 1610 as Great House Farm, prior to conversion into a pub sometime in the eighteenth century. Many tales are told of supernatural activity here, but perhaps the most unusual refers to a certain chair in one of the old meeting rooms at the pub.

In 1791, when Elland Nonconformist community was temporarily left without a minister for its chapel on Jepson Lane, many local denominations were forced to use a meeting room on the upper floor of the pub. These included the United Society of Believers in Christ's Second Appearing – a utopian order colloquially known as the 'Shakers', due to their belief that violent bodily agitation could inspire religion visions. Their ferocious convulsions caused the floor to vibrate to such an extent that the furniture also began to leap and shuffle about. It was said that a certain chair sometimes continued to dance of its own volition long after the sect had moved on.

The most famous apparition associated with The Fleece is surely the gloriously named 'Old Leathery Coit' ('coit' being a phonetic rendering of the dialect pronunciation for 'coat'); a phantom first chronicled in 1901 by Lucy Hamerton. She described him as a headless coachman whose carriage was pulled by two headless horses. They emerged at midnight from a barn on Westgate (now demolished) adjacent to The Fleece, then drove furiously down Dog Lane to Old Earth and back.

The legend was so well known that Elland folk used to say 'there goes Old Leathery Coit' whenever a violent and sudden gust of wind disturbed the night. Although such ghosts are more often rumoured than actually witnessed, Hamerton records that Old Leathery Coit was seen during her lifetime by a couple returning from the house of a sick relative late one night in January – much to their terror.

The story of Old Leathery Coit is sometime conflated with a separate tradition regarding an indelible bloodstain at The Fleece, but this is actually connected with a murder committed at the pub in the nineteenth century. One market day in Elland, a travelling hawker attempted to defraud a local man and, upon discovering the deception, the locals chased the merchant to his accommodation at The Fleece. A struggle ensued and one combatant was stabbed and killed. His grave can be seen in the churchyard at St Mary's nearby – the stone is notable due to its sanctimonious epitaph – commissioned by Revd Christopher Atkinson, an incumbent of the church who often cavilled at The Fleece's rowdiness.

The bloodstain left by the murdered man on the staircase was supposedly impossible to scrub out. During renovations to the pub in 1966, this staircase was removed and placed in storage. It was restored ten years later, although the steps no longer led anywhere, and the bloodstain was placed beneath glass as a feature of interest. Sadly, the relevant stair was mistakenly destroyed by contractors conducting another round of renovation work several years later.

Despite this loss, ghostly activity endures at The Fleece. In 2004, the licensees, Neil and Cassandra Monkman, reported that their pet Doberman behaved very oddly in the bar; then in 2011, Emma Clarke told the local press that she'd experienced a variety of poltergeist activity during her tenure. She reported mysterious knockings at night, several cold spots, and – as with so many pub hauntings – she regularly found glasses inexplicably shattered. Clearly it will take more than the demolition of a barn or staircase to exorcise The Fleece's resident spirits.

## James Street, Elland

The study of ghosts in early folkloristics was biased towards antique and rural traditions believed to hark back to some pre-industrial golden age. However, in recent years, the ghost panics which seized so many urban areas between the eighteenth and the early twentieth century have become a popular area of study. Such flaps were once so common in English towns and cities that the social historian Owen Davies has dubbed them a form of 'urban recreation'. The most famous cases are the many outbreaks of hysteria related to Spring-heeled Jack during the Victorian era, but few settlements of any size were not at some point seized by such an episode.

Elland's urban ghost panic occurred in 1933 and was centred around James Street – then a relatively new residential development near the centre of town, consisting of rows of small terraced houses for the local mill workers. It was predominantly working-class territory and it was amongst such communities that urban ghost panics most typically irrupted nationally. Few nineteenth-century houses survive on James Street today – most have been demolished to make way for modern industrial development – but some surrounding terraces remain intact and offer a decent impression of what the area would have been like in the 1930s.

The flap began on the night of Friday, 3 May 1933 when the residents of James Street were disturbed by the sound of a blood-curdling moan between the hours of 11.30 p.m. and 3 a.m. This uncanny wail recurred on the nights of Tuesday 7th and Friday 10th. Doubtless folk today could think of at least one common nocturnal activity that might cause such a racket, but the 1930s were a more innocent and decorous age. Moreover, those who heard it at the time were adamant that it was not a natural human or animal sound and it caused such consternation amongst the local tenants that one woman had to be pacified with smelling salts.

The sound was described by Mrs Perks, of No. 28 James Street, as 'not like a dog or an owl or an electric hooter. It is a long moaning sound that makes you wonder if someone's in pain somewhere. With it happening at night it makes it sound worse, whatever it is, and the worst of it is not knowing where it comes from

or what it is.' Another told the newspaper reporter, 'You can smile, but you'd be flayed if you heard it.' Several residents attempted to go in search of the source of the disturbance at night but nobody found anything and whilst the police had been informed, they had not reached any conclusions.

Police advice was roundly ignored and following reports in the local press the flap only gained momentum, especially after a journalist cheekily associated the sounds with Elland's most famous spectre – Old Leathery Coit! Until this point only residents of James Street had attempted to locate the source of the midnight moans, but on the two nights following the publication of the newspaper article, their ranks were swelled by sensation-seekers from across the district. It started with local children at around 7 p.m., then as midnight approached, dozens of adults assembled – but the James Street banshee was never heard again.

As one resident put it:

What self-respecting ghost would show itself under such conditions? The main contingent of 'ghost-layers' arrived after 11p.m. and remained there 'til the early hours of the morning. These consisted of about a dozen budding sleuths, together with a few pixies and their fairy godmothers, and they kept up a running commentary the whole time. Later they were joined by a motorcyclist … this one fairly revelled in his duties as, taking a small outside patrol, he reported every few minutes to the headquarters staff with due precision, viz. stop, tootle on the horn, three false starts, and then off with a rush. This continued until they got tired of their self-imposed vigil.

Tag Cut at Cromwell Bottom.

## Tag Cut, Elland

Here a ghost called Old Tag was alleged to inhibit a room called the 'Tag Chamber'. In the early twentieth century, a local man named John Crowther recalled that his grandmother had been a regular guest at at the haunted property a century or so earlier. On one particular night she was woken by an almighty series of crashes sounding from Tag Chamber and never dared to spend a night at the house again.

Old Tag was also supposed to appear from a secret passage as a headless coachman driving two headless horses. This apparition greatly resembles Old Leathery Coit and the two are often confused. However, whilst Leathery Coit rides from Westgate to Old Earth through Elland town centre, Old Tag's peregrinations take him along the southern bank of the River Calder towards Cromwell Bottom.

Legend claims that Old Tag caused a local stone mill to abandon their plans to allow canal freight access to their quarry near Strangstry Wood. Prior to the constructing of the Calder & Hebble Navigation between Brighouse and Elland in 1808, barges often used the River Calder and traversed meanders or rapids by using privately built short stretches of canal called 'cuts'. One such example was built in 1770 but never used; Elland folk claimed the owner of the stone mill was forced to abandon the cut due to Old Tag's nocturnal activity and the stretch of water has since been known as Tag Cut.

A more likely explanation is that it was superseded by the Calder & Hebble Navigation. Despite its disuse, the cut was never backfilled and it has now become part of the Cromwell Bottom Local Nature Reserve due to the unique eco-system sustained by its slow-flowing waters. However, there is an eerie atmosphere about the place: iron-oxide leaches from old mine-workings in the hillside above to stain the water rusty-red and the trees are unusually contorted because they cannot put down roots in the shallow alkaline soil.

Although their routes are different, it seems probable that Old Leathery Coit and Old Tag are what folklorists call allomotifs – narrative variants within the same basic legend. In 1971, a local writer suggested that the headless apparition might represent the ghost of the younger Sir John de Eland who was murdered crossing the River Calder near Elland Bridge. However, whilst Eland's family were associated with Tag Chamber through marriage in the fourteenth century, Sir John resided elsewhere when he was killed. This means there is no reason his restless spirit should be connected with the property and, sadly, whatever origin story may have been attached to Old Tag has been lost.

*Clay House, Greetland.*

## Clay House, Greetland

The four gables of Clay House are a familiar sight overlooking the junction of Stainland and Saddleworth Road at West Vale. Completed in 1661 for the Clay family, the hall and grounds were purchased by Greetland Urban District Council in 1923 for the enjoyment of the local community. Owned by Calderdale Council today, the house itself is hired out for functions and only the park is permanently open to the public.

Clay House is said to be haunted by a spectral 'white lady' called Jane, who wanders its corridors disconsolately weeping. Linda King recalls that her grandfather witnessed the apparition when he dwelt at the hall in the early 1900s and it was seen again in the 1970s by Mr Ronald Innes, a former director of Calderdale Museums who lived in an apartment at Clay House following his retirement.

The ghost was generally identified as a young woman who'd fallen in love with a man 'below her station' and whose family had imprisoned her in a room at Clay House to prevent the couple eloping. Although the legend is not specific, presumably 'Jane' starved or pined to death in this room. Ms King recalls that her grandfather discovered a secret chamber at the hall during his youth but was told to leave it alone, whilst a former district nurse who sometimes worked from Clay House was told that the love-lorn girl had scratched something on a window frame there.

There was certainly a historical Jane Clay, who lived there between 1693 and 1709, but she married twice and so it seems unlikely that she was the source of the legend. Other locals have associated the ghost with 'Mary Clay', who was supposedly jilted at the altar and subsequently committed suicide in the house. This name appears in the historical record – one Mary Clay lived at Clay House sometime during the seventeenth century – but the tradition regarding her abandonment and suicide may be apocryphal.

The grounds of Clay House are also reputedly haunted and in recent years Andy Owens received a report from a woman named Jayne Hewitt regarding her experience there. One wintry evening she was walking her dog on a familiar route in the park when she felt overwhelmed by an unaccountable sense of dread as they neared the house. Turning her gaze to the left, she was confronted by the sight of a person hanging from one of the trees that border the driveway on the left. This image lasted a brief moment and then it vanished.

A similar atmosphere of dread was attached to the same area of the park by Carol McCambridge, who has experienced a recurring nightmare featuring that spot ever since childhood: 'The dreams are always the same: there's coffin after coffin – laid out on the left, where you describe – all open and with bodies in them; I don't always see what's in the coffins, because by this time, I usually wake up in a panic!' Needless to say, Ms McCambridge has never walked her own dog in that region of the grounds.

# 5

# THE RYBURN VALLEY

## The Blue Ball Inn, Soyland

For many years, the site of the remote Blue Ball Inn at Soyland was thought to have been one of the earliest hostelries in the region, owing its position to the Roman road between Manchester and Ilkley. A sign communicating this tradition hung outside the pub at one time. However, whilst the Roman road did run over Blackstone Edge – where it is known as Dhoul's (Devil's) Pavement – it did not pass the location of the Blue Ball. In fact, the inn is more likely to have been converted from weavers' cottages sometime in the eighteenth century.

The name 'Blue Ball' is taken from a common symbol by which publicans once advertised their establishment to a largely illiterate populace. The inn closed its doors to customers in 2002 and the building was converted back into cottages, but a blue ball still hangs from the exterior as a mark of its heritage.

During its lifetime as a pub, the Blue Ball was believed to be haunted by a spirit called Faith, who had worked there as a serving maid in the eighteenth century, under a landlord known as Iron Will. A notorious brigand and lecher,

Iron Will soon turned his lascivious attentions to Faith, but after she rebuffed him, the brute forced himself upon her and left her insensible to drown in a pool on the moors.

Following the discovery of her body, the coroner returned a verdict of suicide. Thus, with her reputation maligned

*The eponymous sign still hangs outside Blue Ball cottages at Soyland.*

and murder unpunished, Faith's angry spirit has haunted the area ever since. Tradition asserts that her panicked cries still echo across the moors; whilst diners at the Blue Ball often heard her desperate footsteps crossing the empty room above – the room that had once been Iron Will's chamber.

It is unclear how reliable this narrative might be. Such stories are often attached to old hostelries across Britain and are frequently little more than a migratory legend, with no foundation in historical fact. Nonetheless, it is instructive that a proclamation was issued on 25 March 1770 for the arrest of sundry individuals known to be involved with the Cragg Vale Coiners, names James Proctor of Blue Ball, Soyland, and Will Proctor, of Maiden Stones (an adjacent farm).

James is recorded as a 'shalloon-maker' at the Blue Ball in 1766, but around 1775, a Brighouse malt-dealer noted that William Proctor owed him £20. Could William Proctor have inherited the hostelry from James and have provided the template for the figure of Iron Will? And if that aspect of the legend is true, how much else might be?

On the other hand, it is curious that the Blue Ball stands so close to a spot called Maiden Stones, which some historians have suggested as the site of a lost prehistoric monument. Perhaps the spectral cries across the moor were originally attributed to some female tutelary spirit of the sort so often associated with ancient remains, only to have been 'rationalised' and conflated with the story of the Blue Ball coiners at a later date.

Certainly Manshead End – the hillside on which the Blue Ball and Maiden Stones are situated – has yielded evidence of continuous occupation from the Mesolithic until the Bronze Age. Sadly, any remains at Maiden Stones have been lost beneath the rising peat, or else destroyed by human activity such as quarrying, leaving its *genius loci* to wander disconsolately across the moor.

Faith's spectre is not the only apparition to have been experienced at the Blue Ball and local paranormal researcher, Andy Owens, reports a quite different encounter. Barman Phil Chappell, and the landlady, Rose Foster, had been enjoying an after-hours nightcap in the otherwise empty pub one night in 1991. As the pair chatted, Chappell looked over and noticed a man propped up against the wall further along the bar. This stranger simply returned the barman's gaze with a smile, before melting into thin air.

It would be tempting to identify this phantom with Iron Will, but Chappell gave no indication that the individual he saw was anachronistically attired: he was simply described as balding, with a black beard, and dressed in an open-necked shirt and dark jacket. Consequently, the identity of the Blue Ball's other resident spook, remains an enigma.

### Height Walk, Ripponden

Two versions of this ghost story exist and have become conflated over the years, possibly as the result of antiquarian fancy. The legend was even incorporated into *Romance of an Old Manor House*, the first novel by forgotten Edwardian children's author, Rowland Walker. Nonetheless, it seems that Madam o' th' Height once represented a very real source of dread for Ryburn folk, who would strenuously avoid the area after dark.

The fullest treatment of the legend was provided by John Longbottom, a local schoolmaster, for the *Halifax Courier* in 1895. According to this account, Madam o' th' Height first manifested around the centenary of the Battle of Marston Moor in 1744.

She was described as 'a lady all dressed in white – a white silk dress. She had a long silver-mounted cane in one hand; a big silver bowl in the other.' The apparition was said to emerge from wainscotting in an old hall, climb the stairs then walk along the gallery and through various rooms. On other occasions, she manifested at the foot of an old apple tree in the garden.

This eighteenth-century legend associated Madam o' th' Height with the mistress of the house during the English Civil Wars, whose husband fought for the Royalists at the Battle of Marsden Moor on 2 July 1644. During his absence, the lady of the house hid all their valuables lest the Parliamentarians come looking for plunder. Unfortunately, she passed away before her husband returned: according to one source, she met her death through gluttony, which doubtless reflects working-class attitudes towards the gentry during the period of the legend's foundation. When she expired, the secret of the whereabouts of the family's heirlooms died with her – including the silver bowl. Her apparition was thought to be trying to lead her descendants towards the horde.

The second legend associates Madam o' th' Height with the unfortunate Charlotte Brisco, illegitimate daughter of Edward Dyne Brisco. Her beloved father died in 1815, aged 37, when Charlotte was still a young girl and owing to an entail on his estate, its ownership could only pass to 'lawfully begotten' descendants. Hence, Charlotte was wrenched from her childhood home and sent to reside with her mother in Wakefield.

As she matured, Miss Brisco came to be known as the most beautiful woman in the city and on 24 January 1827, she married the solicitor, Edward Fenton. Tragically, Fenton died shortly after the union and Charlotte followed him to the grave on 27 December of the same year. Her funeral drew a large crowd of mourners and she was interred in the chancel of Wakefield Cathedral.

Although both Longbottom's Civil War dame and the ill-starred Charlotte Brisco have been associated with the title Madam o' th' Height, they might have been two different apparitions entirely. Whilst both were characterised as white or grey ladies, clad in a long silk dress, their habits and accoutrements seem to have been different.

Longbottom's spectre carried the cane and silver bowl, and seemed primarily to haunt the house and gardens. Conversely, Brisco's shade was usually encountered on Height Walk, the road which runs from the house to St Bartholomew's church in Ripponden – local tradition asserts she searches for the grave of her father who was buried there. She was also said to be accompanied by a large white dog; this may have been a favoured companion in life or a reference to the hunting dogs featured on both the arms and crest of the Brisco family.

Ultimately, it is difficult to establish to whom the title Madam o' th' Height originally referred. The title may have been used for two distinct apparitions, but unfortunately the documentary evidence remains unclear and characteristics of one are often attributed to the other.

The supposed events in the 'Longbottom narrative' predate the 'Brisco narrative' by more than half a century, but as neither seem to have been recorded until the late nineteenth century, it is impossible to establish priority in the oral tradition.

It may be that the Brisco narrative largely superseded the Longbottom narrative in local folklore, but they may also have been developed simultaneously as rival legends to explain the same phenomenon, according to who you asked. For instance, one might have been a Brisco family legend and the other a topic of tavern talk. It is curious, however, that when a local farmer was renovating the hall on behalf of Sir Musgrave Horton Brisco, he discovered a hidden recess behind the wainscotting. Contained within was an ancient oak board inscribed with the eerie legend, 'In this tormenting place we are forc'd to stay and …' before tailing off into mystery.

## No. 59 Towngate, Sowerby

Situated on a hillside above the confluence of the Rivers Calder and Ryburn, Sowerby is an older settlement than its upstart sibling, Sowerby Bridge, nestling in the valley below. Whilst the latter did not flourish until the Industrial Revolution, Sowerby is recorded in Domesday Book and once boasted a Norman motte-and-bailey castle, which survives only as an earthwork on the north side of Towngate.

The southern edge of this thoroughfare is dominated by social housing and although the current blocks were clearly constructed during the 1960s, earlier dwellings on the site were also municipally owned, including an old semi-detached cottage numbered 57 and 59. In the winter of 1954–55, the latter became the scene of a well-attested and highly publicised poltergeist haunting.

The case was first reported in the *Yorkshire Evening Post* on 18 February 1955, which told how the Polish immigrant, Bogdan Tarandzief, his wife Doreen (née Georgeson) and their 18-month-old daughter, Kateryna, had been forced to abandon their home at No. 59 Towngate by phenomena including 'terrible rushing noises, footsteps, doors that refuse to stay closed, jangling pots in the kitchen, bangs in the back bedroom and in fact everything that goes bump in the night'.

The family claimed they had been unable to enjoy a full night's rest since October the previous year and only returned to the house for their evening meal. Bogdan had been forced to spend a further 15s a week on lodgings in Halifax, whilst his wife and daughter returned to sleep in her parents' house.

Although Doreen Tarandzief claimed the family had never seen anything, her father, Gordon Georgeson, described investigating No. 59 one night:

> I took Lassie with me, suddenly she leaped and whined in terrible fright. I saw a sudden glow, a glow of golden light coming apparently from down the bedroom stairs. At other times I have been told of lights in the house in the early hours but … so far as I known there was no-one in the house.

Herbert and Mary Smithson, the tenants of No. 57 next door, also collaborated events: 'We have heard strange noises from next door for a long time

… The noises have gone on since they decided to sleep somewhere else, sometimes there are banging noises and the jangling of pots at one o' clock in the morning.'

As tenants of the local authority, the Tarandziefs initially contacted the Sowerby Bridge Urban District Council, whose inspectors were unable to find anything that might account for the disturbances. By this time, local gossips had begun to speculate that the Tarandziefs were fabricating the whole affair in order to secure a better council house. It is a common accusation levelled against social housing tenants who report such phenomena.

Others have taken a more subtle approach, suggesting that a tenant's perception that their house is haunted may be an unconscious response to their environment. More than one folklorist has interpreted hauntings reported in rented accommodation as the tenant projecting their alienation from a house that is not their own onto an external agency such as a ghost.

In this instance, however, the testimony of independent witnesses suggests that the phenomena was objective and soon the attendant publicity began to attract numerous 'experts' hoping to study it. It began with Jack Quain, a local electrician and water-diviner, who held a vigil at the house on the night of 19 February.

During his watch, Quain reported that the wall between No. 59 and the adjoining house was vibrating so powerfully that it snapped his whalebone dowsing rod when he attempted to press it against the surface. Quain was followed by a group of mediums from Keighley, the home town of Spiritualism in Britain, who claimed that the trouble was caused by Bogdan's late mother attempting to contact her son from beyond the veil.

The haunting was eventually brought to the attention of other investigators, albeit more than a year after the last activity had been reported, when Frank Pearson, a member of the Society for Psychical Research living near Huddersfield, contacted the respected parapsychologists Eric J. Dingwall and Trevor H. Hall, inviting their opinions on the case.

The pair visited Sowerby on 26 June 1956, by which time both No. 59 and No. 57 had been abandoned. Nonetheless, their trip was not in vain. They observed evidence of recent subsidence at the property, including a substantial settlement crack, and obtained intelligence regarding an old culvert which ran downhill from the site of the old castle, beneath Towngate in the direction of No. 59.

With this information, they concluded that 'in very wet weather a considerable force of water would come down the hill and might exert pressure on the subsoil and foundations of houses built over and near the end of the conduit, causing slight movements of structure'.

If this hypothesis is well founded, it would explain the signs of subsidence at No. 59 Towngate and the curious rushing noises which the occupiers are reported to have heard in the kitchen on the ground floor. Although the Tarandziefs had lived at No. 59 for three years before they noticed any disturbance, Hall and Dingwall suggested that excessive rainfall in the autumn of 1954 and heavy snow in February 1955 stimulated the phenomenon over that period.

As Trevor H. Hall was a chartered surveyor in his professional life, it may seem that his opinion on structural matters cannot be taken lightly. However, work by the parapsychologists Alan Gauld and Tony Cornell in the 1970s suggested that this geophysical theory of hauntings was problematic. They demonstrated experimentally that even extreme vibrations, sufficient to seriously destabilise the fabric of the building, were not able to cause much noticeable movement of objects within.

Nonetheless, in the wake of the Tarandziefs' experiences, the local authority evidently concluded that Nos 57 and 59 Towngate were unfit for human habitation and after several years left vacant – a source of terror to local children – the properties were demolished.

## The Travellers' Rest, Sowerby

Despite being named as one of *The Times'* top ten countryside restaurants in 2007, due to the glorious views from its remote position above Sowerby, this former gastropub has gone the way of so many hostelries in Calderdale and closed its doors for good. Following its demise in 2011, the building was converted into separate residential houses.

However, in the summer of 1983, when it was still a thriving local institution, the Travellers' Rest was involved in a unique poltergeist case – one which spanned the Continent and made the lives of two men a misery. The haunting is unusual in that it was focused on individuals, rather than a location; but although the disturbances seemed to have their origin in the South Aegean, the Travellers' Rest became the scene of much unnerving phenomena.

In July 1983, a 42-year-old barman, referred to as Henry in the original reports, travelled with his friend, Alan, to the Greek island of Mykonos, where they'd booked eleven days in a newly built apartment. Soon, they began to notice that they were not alone; they found pans of water boiling on the stove, candles burning in empty rooms and the table regularly set for three people.

At first, they assumed the landlord must have employed a cleaner to make their stay more comfortable. However, when they discovered candles newly lit in rooms they had only left a moment ago, without a match in sight, the pair grew increasingly puzzled. As the incidents were of a minor nature, they were not too perturbed and when they left they jokingly bid farewell to their spectral flatmate. It responded by hurling an ashtray from the dressing table with such force that it hit the ceiling.

But the spirit was not done with them. From that point, the disturbances grew increasing inconvenient and aggressive. In the taxi to the airport, the entity tore open a sachet of sugar in their luggage, showering the vehicle's interior with the contents. Then, during their flight home, postcards and a bottle of sun lotion erupted from their bags over fellow passengers.

Even when they got back to the security of their own homes in England, Henry and Alan were not free of the phenomena. They continued to find candles lit without explanation, whilst books were thrown off shelves and pictures fell violently from the walls. On one occasion, they found one of their settees had been turned on end during the night and on another they woke to find a wardrobe had been dragged across the room in which they were sleeping.

Travellers Cottages (formerly the Travellers' Rest) at Sowerby.

Henry lived in a flat above the Travellers' Rest, where he worked as a barman, and landlord Peter Rogal witnessed strange activity himself. 'It was strongest when the two of them were together,' he observed, 'It was a very strange situation. Coins have slid about and pictures have moved. One or two customers reported that coins had hit them.'

Showers of coins became a regular occurrence in Alan and Henry's presence, but whilst the pair found this merely inconvenient and embarrassing, the poltergeist's mischief could be much more threatening. Henry returned to his flat one day to find a black triangle daubed on his mirror and a knife thrust into the kitchen table. He even claimed to have been kicked and slapped on his back by the entity.

Perhaps most perplexing were the changes wrought on a photograph the men had taken of the kitchen of their apartment on Mykonos. The perspective had altered, and the scene now included a lit candle, along with a sinister shrouded figure sat at the table. Like the eponymous print in M.R. James' acclaimed ghost story, *The Mezzotint*, the photo continued to undergo changes – sometimes several in a single night. Independent witnesses corroborated these transformations and even signed the back of the photo to ensure that no trickery was taking place.

A representative from the respected Institute of Psychophysical Research later commented:

> This is a remarkable case because of the frequency of the incidents and because the incidents themselves are extraordinary. The two men's accounts have corresponded exactly. They would have to have gone to great lengths to make it all up … and we are taking their claims very seriously.

Eventually, the two men grew so disturbed by the protean image that they burnt it and placed the debris in a dustbin; Henry later found its charred remnants on his floor, prompting him to flush it down the toilet. At his wits' end one night, Henry asked the entity if it wanted exorcising, to which it replied by shattering a crystal decanter.

The pair subsequently took advice from a Spiritualist medium and attempted to rid themselves of the troublesome spirit by writing a note requesting that it depart, then leaving a pen beside the paper so it could respond. As soon as they'd composed their message, a picture flew from the wall, causing them to flee room. When they returned, a 'spidery scrawl' had appeared on the paper beneath their own inscription. It simply read: 'Help.'

Although they could not really afford it, this entreaty persuaded Henry and Alan to return to the apartment in Mykonos, where they again asked the presence to depart and, on the medium's recommendation, left behind some personal tokens such as a handkerchief and cufflinks.

Whilst on the island, the pair spoke to the apartment's landlord and perhaps gleaned some information relevant to their experiences. He told them that shortly before their original stay, workmen constructing a new villa on adjacent land had excavated an old well in the garden, at the bottom of which they found a body. The remains had been reburied during the same week that Henry and Alan had rented the apartment. 'Why the spirit chose us, I will never know,' Henry commented, 'I just hope it is now at rest.'

## The Rushcart Inn, Sowerby

Formerly known as the Star Inn, this public house at the centre of the Sowerby was renamed following the revival of rushbearing at Sowerby Bridge. Rushbearing was originally an ecclesiastic tradition, possibly dating from the Middle Age, which survived in many places until the early twentieth century. The custom predated the installation of pews in many churches and its original purpose was to collect rushes from the surrounding hills with which to strew the church floor – thereby providing warmer, more comfortable seating on the stone or even dirt floor of the church through winter.

The pub is reputedly haunted by a character named John 'Almighty' Whiteley, who in 1810 married Alice Jennings, widow of the man who'd built the establishment in 1798. Whitely was an eccentric fellow who was variously employed as a woollen spinner, an auctioneer, an author, a lay preacher and a policeman. Although he was often in trouble with the law himself, Whiteley called himself the 'Lynx-Eyed Thief-Catcher' and attempts were made on his life by local criminals. Meanwhile, as a lay preacher he would deliver sermons from an old postbox converted into a pulpit in an upper room at the pub – sometimes to a drunken congregation.

Sadly, Whiteley fell on hard times following the death of his much older wife; and he was forced to sell the inn to cover his debts in 1849. His liability was such that he was placed in the workhouse at Mill Bank and when he died – seven years later on 6 April 1858 – he was buried in an unmarked grave at the local church. His surviving legacy at the

Star Inn (as it was then known) was a large portrait which once hung in the tap room and seemed to be accompanied by Whiteley's ghostly presence.

During the 1950s and 1960s, an array of poltergeist phenomena was reported from the pub; including the sound of singing for which no source could be found and doors which opened and closed of their own accord. Meanwhile, the portrait of John Whiteley so disturbed customers – who claimed its eyes followed them around the room – that it was placed in an outhouse for storage.

Whenever the landlord attempted to rehang the painting, the paranormal activity flared up again. It was later hung in the offices of Whitaker's Brewery in Halifax and auctioned off when the firm closed in 1969. However, the removal of the picture did not quell the haunting entirely; when Eddie and Christine Mallerby took the license of the hostelry in 1989, they were so disturbed by a sensation of presence – such as being watched and followed around the building – that they moved on the following year.

Surprisingly, the portrait turned up in an edition of the *Antiques Roadshow* broadcast from Arundel Castle in September 2007. The owner, Allan Kenny, complained that his family experienced a cold spot in the vicinity of the painting whilst they were often plagued by kinetic activity such as glass frames shattering mysteriously and door latches rattling open in the middle of the night.

The Rushcart Inn (formerly the Star) at Sowerby.

Most sinisterly, Mr Kenny claimed that when their baby daughter was asleep in her cot – directly below the painting – he and his wife often heard the sound of somebody softly singing Brahms' lullaby through the baby monitor. On one occasion, Mrs Kenny had heard the singing whilst her husband had been stood on the upstairs landing outside the room and could hear nothing.

Although the Kenny family initially dismissed this as radio interference, the auditory phenomena took on an even more disturbing character when the family were contacted by Patricia Parry. Parry's father had owned the Star Inn between 1959 and 1960: the period in which the original supernatural activity had been recorded in connection with the portrait. In 1960, Parry gave birth to a daughter whilst she was living at the pub. Tragically the child died, but during her brief lifetime her favourite toy was a teddy bear that had played Brahms lullaby.

# 6

# LUDDENDEN DEAN, MYTHOLMROYD & CRAGG VALE

### The Lord Nelson, Luddenden

Perched beside a hairpin bend on Luddenden's steep and narrow high street, this fine building was erected in 1634, originally as a private dwelling. It was possibly once the home of Catholic recusants, as there is evidence of a priest hole which was formerly connected to the churchyard by a secret tunnel running behind the lounge wall. Fragments of ecclesiastical architecture have also been found in the building; perhaps hidden there from the iconoclastic depredations of Roundheads during the English Civil Wars.

The building was converted into a pub sometime in the eighteenth century and was initially called the White Swan; only to be patriotically renamed following Lord Nelson's victory at the Battle of Trafalgar in 1805. Somewhat incongruously, an upper room in the hostelry became home to Calderdale's earliest public lending library in 1776, thanks to a donation of around 1,000 books by a former vicar of the church.

Buildings of this vintage often have a ghost attached and the Lord Nelson is no exception. Reports suggest that the phenomena is mostly confined to low-level poltergeist activity: throwing glasses from the shelves or pictures from the wall, and unnerving the staff with a vague sense of 'presence'. Like so many other tavern spirits, it apparently also delights in tampering with the beer taps – in 2005 the landlord complained he had to turn them back on weekly.

Its most striking habit, however, is playing notes on a piano situated in the bar. The instrument stands in the recess left by a substantial old fireplace, only recently uncovered after having been walled up for many years. It is tempting to associate this event with the paranormal phenomena, which often seems to be correlated with structural alterations.

Seemingly the phenomena has not yet been personified and no name is attached to it. Nonetheless, one candidate can surely not be ignored; namely Branwell Brontë, the even less fortunate brother of the famed literary sisters and the Lord Nelson's most notorious customer.

Despite early promise as a portrait artist and poet, Branwell's career foundered on the rocks of drunkenness, debt and sexual scandal. He succumbed

*The Lord Nelson, Luddenden.*

wholly to alcoholism and opiate addiction towards the end of life; delirium tremens probably hastened his death from tuberculosis in 1848, aged only 31.

Branwell began to patronise the Lord Nelson in 1841, having managed to secure a job as 'clerk-in-charge' at Luddendenfoot railway station. He remained a regular at the inn – even reserving a favourite chair in a corner of the bar – until he was dismissed from his job at the station on 4 March 1842 for 'gross misconduct' and 'culpable negligence', charges relating to his persistent drunkenness on duty and poor accounting.

He later wrote about his time at Luddendenfoot, 'I would rather give my hand than undergo again the grovelling carelessness, the malignant yet cold debauchery, the determination to find how far mind could carry body without both being chucked into hell, which too often marked my conduct there'.

Prone to such bouts of self-recrimination, yet often possessed by a stubbornness which drove him to defy his demons, there is perhaps no more likely place for the restless spirit of Branwell Brontë to haunt than Luddenden and the Lord Nelson Inn, scene of one of his lowest ebbs.

## Kershaw House, Luddendenfoot

Kershaw at Luddendenfoot is first recorded in the Wakefield Court Rolls for 1307 as 'Kirkshaugh', meaning 'church copse'. It is unclear, however, to which church this refers, as no record of a place of worship in Luddenden Dean during this period has ever been found. Nonetheless, Kershaws' ecclesiastic associations seem to have remained strong over the centuries, and this toponymic connection with pre-Reformation worship may account for a legend which has attached itself to the seventeenth-century house now standing on the site.

Local tradition claims that during the post-Reformation persecution of Catholics in England, two nuns were hung from a tree at Kershaw, before being beheaded, then drawn and quartered. It is said that once a year, on the anniversary of their execution, their headless spectres can be seen riding a phantom coach up Luddenden Dean towards Kershaw.

Some corroboration of this legend is supposedly provided by the priest hole which can be found in the double-storied porch on the west wing of Kershaw House. However, the actual evidence for this is problematic.

It is true that Kershaw House as it stands today was built during the seventeenth century by James Murgatroyd of East Riddlesden Hall near Keighley (to which Kershaw House bears a number of architectural similarities). A wealthy cloth manufacturer, James Murgatroyd was also one of the most prominent Catholics in the district and – as punitive measures against 'Popish' recusants had only grown stricter since the Gunpowder Plot of

*Kershaw House, Luddendenfoot.*

1605 – a priest hole would undoubtedly have been a wise precaution.

Nonetheless, there is no historical record of any Catholic priests being discovered at Kershaw House and subsequently executed, let alone nuns. Indeed, only one nun was ever executed for treason in this country; in 1534, during the very earliest days of the English Reformation, after which no female monastic communities survived. In fact, women were rarely hanged or beheaded – they were typically quartered and then burnt.

As such, the story of the headless nuns cannot preserve the memory of any historical event, although it may have arisen as a confused reflection of the connection between Catholicism and Kershaw House in the local collective memory.

It should also be noted that the 'phantom coach' motif is a common migratory legend in England. As folklorist Christina Hole writes, 'Sometimes it comes to fetch away the dying; sometimes ... the already dead use it in their perambulations about the roads and fields of their old home ... It is always black, and so are the driver and his horses. Often both are headless. It appears suddenly on the roadway and moves very fast and usually without noise ...'

## The Grove Inn, Brearley

A familiar landmark on the busy A646 between Mytholmroyd and Luddendenfoot, this terrace of three-storey buildings was originally constructed around 1830 as part of The Grove Brewery, whose name can still be seen inscribed above an archway at the centre of the row.

When the business merged with Whitaker's in 1906, their original home was no longer needed and the terrace was converted into separate buildings; three became private residences, but the site's brewing heritage was preserved by The Grove Inn.

During the 1970s, staff and patrons alike experienced unaccountable sensory phenomena in The Grove, especially a strong smell of bacon and eggs when nobody was cooking – an odour which would disperse as suddenly as it had appeared.

More disturbingly, several people sensed an uncanny presence in the vaulted cellar. Sandra Gelder, the landlady in 1972, reported that she was too afraid to descend into the underground chamber, whilst one man was forced to make a hasty exit after finding himself overwhelmed by the atmosphere. Moreover, customers often complained of feeling an invisible form push past them as they stood at one end of the bar, near to the steps that led below.

Tradition amongst regulars at The Grove attributed the phenomena to a spirit called 'Hilda', who'd worked in the establishment when it had still been attached to the brewery, regularly cooking breakfast for the workers next door. One day she descended into the cellar on an errand, never to be seen again. Although Hilda's body was never discovered, the regulars imagined that she must have fallen into a well in the middle of the cellar floor.

At 35ft deep, the well was certainly a substantial hazard. When a reporter for the *Halifax Courier* was shown the shaft in 1972, it was secured with a heavy iron cover, but it may originally have been used as a convenient water source by the brewery and left accessible.

*The former Grove Inn at Brearley.*

Unfortunately, like so many of Calderdale's most distinctive pubs in recent years, The Grove closed permanently in 2008 and the building faces conversion into apartments. It is not clear what might become of the treacherous well, or the ghost that calls it home.

But perhaps Hilda's presence has now faded. In 2001, almost thirty years after the initial publicity, the latest licensees, Ken and Carol Wheatcroft, were asked if they'd experienced anything unusual in the pub – and although Ken complained that beer taps in the cellar regularly turned themselves on when the pub was empty, they both denied ever smelling that inexplicable aroma of bacon and eggs which had been so strongly associated with Hilda's presence by his predecessors.

## Broadbottom, Mytholmroyd

Described by English Heritage as 'a rare and important survival', a timber-framed dwelling is first recorded at Broadbottom in 1250. This structure was cased in stone in the sixteenth century and although the building was substantially rebuilt in 1844, it is probable that some of the original timber remains within its fabric.

Part of the building is supposed to have been used as a private chapel in the fifteenth century and that ruinous wing long exerted a fascination over local curiosity seekers. In 1906, one visitor wrote:

> This part of the building has a very weird aspect even in broad daylight … It has only one window and the door is always kept locked. The beams and boards are black rotten and hang

*Broadbottom on the hillside above Mytholmroyd.*

down with a very ragged appearance. The floor has almost crumbled away and bears evidence of the accumulation of dust and cobwebs for a few centuries.

In local folklore, the hall is associated with the headless ghost of Old Mayroyd, who rides a spectral white horse from Mayroyd near Hebden Bridge, up the hill to Broadbottom and back again. But whilst Old Mayroyd exists primarily as a legend, the 25-year-old Lavena Saltonstall and her two friends observed more concrete phenomena in the chapel itself on their visit in 1906.

A prolific correspondent of the local newspapers, Saltonstall reported:

We were looking through the window and wondering what the old kist in the corner contained. One of my friends, in a spirit of fun, entreated the ghosts and goblins to come forth. Of course we all laughed, but only for a minute, for immediately a very thin streak of light appeared above the kist and gradually grew bigger until it formed a bright light about nine inches square. It stayed there for about six seconds when it suddenly vanished.

The friends concluded that the ghostly light surely had some unnatural origin: nobody could've been in the room above because the floor was collapsing and, although there were rumours of secret tunnels leading from Broadbottom, the friends had not observed any portal that might give access to these subterranean passages.

A few weeks later, one of the party returned to Broadbottom to investigate further. The student again invited the ghost to appear, and sure enough, a light materialised above the kist for a few seconds before disappearing.

'It was not ordinary light,' the witness insisted. 'It looked just like a woman wearing a robe of some kind of lustrous metallic material.' It is worth noting here that some modern paranormal researchers such as Paul Devereux speculate that rare geophysical phenomena dubbed 'earthlights' may be the cause of many ghost sightings, especially those of the ubiquitous 'white lady'.

## Cragg Vale

Today, Cragg Vale is known as a picturesque tributary of Calderdale, but it was not always so bucolic. Like much of the region, through the Industrial Revolution until the early twentieth century the narrow floor of the valley was crammed with textiles mills, choking the air and polluting its becks.

Working conditions were especially poor. A local minister wrote regarding child labour in Cragg Vale, 'If there is one place in England that needed legislative interference it is this place; for they work 15 and 16 hours a day frequently, and sometimes all night. Oh! it is a murderous system and the mill owners are the pest and disgrace of society.'

One of the most notorious employers was the miserly Hinchcliffe, who lived in a grand residence. Originally built in 1617, the property had to be substantially reconstructed in 1837 by a Halifax worthy named Christopher Rawson, who had purchased it in a dilapidated state. It is not clear why its previous owners had allowed the pile to fall into such disrepair during the eighteenth century, although,

a tragic legend attached to the house may offer some answers.

The tradition was documented in 1882 by a local antiquarian and poet by the name of F.C. Spenser, who turned the narrative into a ballad. Whilst he may have exercised a degree of literary license in its retelling, certain customs still observed by residents of the valley suggest the basic story had been preserved by Cragg Vale folk for generations.

At an unspecified date in the late seventeenth or early eighteenth century, the scion of the owners was a knavish individual, more interested in womanising and gambling than his responsibilities as an heir of the landed gentry. When his parents were away – as they often were, tending distant parts of their estate – the building became the setting for reckless hunts and lavish feasting.

During one such bacchanal, he took advantage of a young, fair-haired maid employed in service at the house and shortly thereafter the girl found that she was pregnant. She confronted him and although he was already engaged to lady of his own social class, he promised to marry the maid.

This commitment was only intended to buy him time to think, and when the maid next pressed him on the matter, in a small sewing room above the porch, the villain silenced her for ever more. He interred his victim's remains in nearby Burnt Wood later that night – yet from that moment, he knew no peace.

His troubles began with a gamekeeper called Morley, who had seen him dispose of the body and proceeded to blackmail his employer until one day, Morley's broken body was discovered at the foot of a gritstone outcrop in Withens Clough.

The villain's other persecutor, however, was less easily shaken off. A light began to shine in that empty chamber above the porch, its flame guttering always towards Burnt Wood; whilst in the small hours, he often felt a clammy hand at his neck and heard a disembodied voice calling his name. His terror was such that he was finally driven from Cragg Vale.

It is said the unfortunate maid haunted the property for forty years, a period equal to what would've been the remainder of her natural life, after which she was finally granted peace and her spirit departed. Despite this conclusion, the maid's ghostly influence is still feared in Cragg Vale and Calderdale folklorist, John Billingsley, has heard the story related orally in the district on a number of occasions over the years.

Nor is her spirit necessarily considered at rest by natives of the vale. Farmers there are reluctant to start haymaking in the top field, where they believed the maid's remains are buried, claiming she would be displeased and send a month's rain to spoil their harvest. In 1981, the *Hebden Bridge Times* reported that the superstition was still observed by Hubert and Annie Haigh of Great House Farm.

The newspaper also spoke to Eileen Ackernley, who had lived at the haunted property since 1954. She claimed to have often heard pattering feet along its corridors and seen her Boxer dogs raise their hackles at some invisible source. More substantially, she had been told that two women collecting for charity once called at the hall in her absence, and when their knocks received no reply, they peered through a downstairs window – only to see a strange golden-haired girl warming herself by the fire.

# 7

# THE UPPER CALDER VALLEY

## Mayroyd, Hebden Bridge

The ancient area of Hebden Bridge known as Mayroyd occupies the north bank of the River Calder on the eastern approach to the town centre. Whilst a dwelling has stood on the site since at least 1399, the building in question was constructed in the early seventeenth century by William Cockcroft, whose family name remained closely associated with it in the local memory. The last member of the family to live there was another William Cockcroft, a well-known local solicitor, who died in 1773.

During the latter half of the seventeenth century, the Nonconformist preacher, Revd Oliver Heywood, referred to the 'debauchery' of the Cockcrofts in his diaries. The precise nature of their activities is left unspecified, and although it did not usually take much to provoke censure from Heywood, it is perhaps the memory of such behaviour that birthed the figure of Old Mayroyd in the popular imagination.

The poet William Dearden recalled in a note to his 1837 publication, *The Star Seeker*, that:

Old Mayroyd's ghost is said to appear every Christmas morn, long before the day, riding upon a white horse, without a head, up and down the valley of Caldene. When I was a boy, I remember rising at the stated hour of his peregrinations to gain a sight of him; but … the old gentleman preferred to remain in unknown seclusion.

Unfortunately, however, Dearden did not record with whom the ghost was identified or why his spirit was restless.

Even the exact route of Old Mayroyd's charge is disputed. One source asserts that he rode up the hill towards

*Hebden Bridge over Mayroyd Canal.*

Broadbottom above Mytholmroyd and back again; another that he rode past a great yew tree in the grounds of Mytholm Hall (also briefly owned by the Cockcrofts) to Milkinbrigg – an eighteenth-century packhorse bridge over the Colden Water in Eaves Wood. A further account asserts that the phantom rode across a bridge over the Rochdale Canal and disappeared into the wheelhouse of Mayroyd Mill.

Curiously, Stephen Wade collected a report of an uncanny experience that occurred in the 1960s at the historic signal box on the eastern side of Hebden Bridge railway station. Although this lies across the river from Mayroyd Mill and Wade does not make the connection with Mayroyd himself, its proximity cannot be ignored.

Wade relates that a signalman named Philip Bolton was working a Sunday night shift when he saw 'a figure in white … it was "brilliant", first hanging around outside his box, and then reappearing at the top of the stairs'. Bolton fled to the toilets and when he returned it had vanished. Two years later, he met another signalman who'd experienced a similar phenomenon on the same shift and was so unnerved by the occurrence that he resigned the next morning. Whilst these apparitions do not resemble Dearden's phantom horseman, they nonetheless confirm Mayroyd as an 'active' area.

The old hall itself was also thought to be haunted and for a period starting on 21 May 1859, the residents were ceaselessly troubled by 'unaccountable noises' emanating from the roof. The *Hebden Bridge & Todmorden Historical Almanac* recalled the affair in 1888: 'There was a boggart at Mayroyd, that kept up a knocking and a banging through the

night, and disturbed the people of the house a good while. But it went away after they'd drilled some holes in the underdrawing. And now they wonder if it was there at all.'

## Church of St Thomas à Becket, Heptonstall

At the heart of the Heptonstall stands the village's most distinctive landmark: the stark shell of the church of St Thomas à Becket. It was originally constructed in 1260, deliberately squat to withstand the hilltop storms – John Wesley, the founder of Methodism and a regular visitor to the village, described it as 'the ugliest [church] I know' in 1786 – but this contingency ultimately proved no match for the elements. Shattered by a great storm in September 1847, the building was abandoned and a new church built alongside.

The ruin is complemented by a teeming churchyard, so densely packed with the dead that its central feature resembles a skeleton adrift on a sea of gravestones. It said that over 100,000 folk are buried there, most notoriously, 'King' David Hartley, executed chief of the Cragg Vale Coiners.

At the southern perimeter of the churchyard, the upper storey of an old cottage backs onto its elevated precincts. This building was formerly the cemetery's ossuary – where old human remains, unearthed during the course of subsequent burials, were deposited. The structure is dated 1779 and at some point it was presumably deconsecrated and turned into a private residence, albeit one whose macabre history was preserved in its fabric.

*Church of St Thomas à Beckett at Heptonstall.*

During renovation work conducted by Jack Smith in 1965, all manner of sepulchral detritus was uncovered: fragments of tombstone had been incorporated into the walls, two grave slabs served as windowsills and a staircase was found to have been constructed from coffin lids. Meanwhile, human remains abounded – shards of bone seemed to come blossoming forth from cracks in the masonry or beneath paved floors.

The refurbishments also revealed a blocked doorway, beyond which a room had lain undisturbed for many years. It was the ensuing restoration that served as a catalyst for the haunting. Perhaps a supernatural presence had caused that chamber to be sealed originally, or perhaps the structural alterations invoked something dormant within the stone.

Both Jack Smith and his contractors reported seeing an apparition, although they witnessed only its feet, sandals and tunic. Such garb loosely suggesting an ecclesiastic of the old religion, the phantom was promptly dubbed a 'monk' by local commentators.

With such an abundance of corpses in both the structure and immediate vicinity, speculation as to the identity of its ghost seems an insuperable task. Nonetheless, there is at least one historical episode and attendant oral tradition that may be significant.

An entry in the Registers of the Archbishops of York records that in December 1482, the church at Heptonstall was temporarily closed for restoration after having been 'polluted by an effusion of blood'. Unfortunately, the actual circumstances behind this extraordinary state of affairs were not documented; but where a reliable primary source does not exist, folklore is so often ready to fill the vacuum.

Above: *Chantry House at Heptonstall.*

Right: *Apotropaic stone head on the church wall at Heptonstall.*

Village legend maintains that the spilt blood belonged to a parish priest, murdered in the church by the disapproving father of a bride whose secret wedding the unfortunate cleric had just consecrated. An echo of the fate of the church's patron, St Thomas à Becket, can be detected, but this does not necessarily invalidate the story's claim to accuracy – after all, it is a matter of historical record that many clergymen have been slain in churches over the centuries and such synchronicities may therefore naturally arise.

Interestingly, it seems that earlier generations in Heptonstall may have been aware of the location's uncanny influence. Set into the churchyard wall adjacent the building, on a level at which many people will fail to notice, there is a crudely carved stone face. Such images are ubiquitous in Calderdale and the majority seem to have been carved between the sixteenth and nineteenth century. Dubbed 'archaic stone heads' by folklorist John Billinglsey, their deliberately stylised primitivism and the contexts in which they appear suggests they were not intended as decorative features. Rather, they seem to have been intended as apotropaic (magically protective) devices, defending a place from misfortune and malefic spiritual forces. Archaic stone heads are often encountered at threshold locations, such as doorways, gateways, gables, bridges or boundary walls – 'liminal' points which to the pre-modern mind represented a border not just between spaces in the physical world, but between this world and the Other.

Few places fulfil such a definition more plainly than the enclosing wall of a churchyard as it meets with the charnel house. Perhaps it is not surprising that, around the time of the haunting, residents recall that dogs balked at the approach along Church Lane and stubbornly refused to cross the threshold.

## The Dog & Partridge, Heptonstall

Although the small village retains two pubs today, Heptonstall once had a much greater number of such establishments, to cater for its larger population. Amongst these was the Dog & Partridge, which occupied a building at Towngate – now a private residence. Its license was withdrawn over a century ago, on 10 October 1889, following a tragic incident which permanently tarnished the pub's reputation in the local psyche.

On the afternoon of 8 August 1889, a Mytholmroyd stonemason named William Clarke began drinking at the Dog & Partridge with his brother Thomas. They were later joined by several woman, including the landlady, Sally Hollinrake ('Sally a' th' Dog'), along with Sally Clegg ('Sally i' th' Garret'), Nellie Fearby and Emily Clark. As the day wore on, Thomas left, whilst William and three of the women proceeded to occupy an upstairs room where, according to Sally Hollinrake's testimony, 'some jollifaction' took place.

Furley House, formerly the Dog & Partridge, at Heptonstall.

The women left William Clarke in a drunken stupor at about 7 p.m., but a couple of hours later he summoned enough wherewithal to descend into the bar and devour some veal pie with a noggin of whisky. Clarke then returned upstairs to a small chamber connected to the main bedroom and passed out in a chair. He was last seen in this condition around 10.30 p.m.

Only an hour later, he was found severely injured in the street outside the Dog & Partridge, having apparently fallen from the attic window of the pub. William Clarke died in the early hours of the following morning, but not before he had been able to tell his brother, Thomas, that the last thing he could remember was feeling somebody rifle through his pockets before being knocked senseless by a blow to the stomach.

Several days later, Sally Hollinrake handed Clarke's watch to the police, claiming that he had asked her to 'look after it' for him; whilst at the subsequent inquest into the death one witness claimed to have heard William shout, 'Oh Sally, tha' shouldn't ha' done that!' shortly before the time of his fall. Further suspicion of foul play was provoked by the observation that to have fallen or thrown himself from the attic window, Clarke would have needed to cross the main bedroom and climb the attic steps, thereby disturbing Hollinrake's family.

Yet despite such persuasive evidence, the coroner's jury returned an open verdict – indicating that although the death appeared suspicious, no firm conclusion could be reached. It is an adjudication most commonly reached in cases of suicide where the victim's intent cannot be proved. However, this outcome did not satisfy the public mood, and the crowd who had assembled outside the Black Bull in Hebden Bridge – where the inquest had taken place – erupted into a riot. Even the local newspaper published a trenchant denunciation of the proceedings.

It seems likely that the closure of the Dog & Partridge so shortly after these events reflected the hostility the local populace came to feel towards the pub and its landlady. Nonetheless, this comeuppance may not have been sufficient to appease William Clarke's unavenged spirit.

By the early 1960s, the building was occupied by the family of local artist Geoffrey Coning – including his teenage stepson Peter Harvey. Harvey told paranormal researcher Stephen Wade that around 1963 he had experienced a variety of weird phenomena in his attic bedroom there, the window of which William Clarke had fallen or been pushed from almost three-quarters of a century earlier.

Although he was not initially aware of its history, Harvey recalled that the room always had a disquieting atmosphere. At night, he was often disturbed by disembodied groans and the creak of floorboards – almost as if something was being dragged across them. He even began to believe the attic was 'hexed' following a series of accidents, which culminated in his fall down the staircase, breaking his leg. When Harvey later heard the story of William Clarke's grievous misadventure, he found the implications horribly clear.

## Lumb Falls & Abel Cross, Crimsworth Dean

A narrow tributary of Hebden Dale, Crimsworth Dean joins the valley at Midgehole, near the foot of the famous local beauty spot, Hardcastle Crags. Whilst Crimsworth Dean is perhaps less frequented than its neighbour, it is no less numinous. The poet, Ted Hughes, who spent his first seven years living in Mytholmroyd, referred to the dean as 'a sacred space for me'. He invoked his childhood haunt in a number of poems, and his short ghost story, 'The Deadfall', was inspired by his own quasi-shamanic experience on a camping expedition there as a boy.

Crimsworth Dean's centrepiece is undoubtedly Lumb Hole, where an early eighteenth-century packhorse bridge crosses one of the most captivating waterfalls in West Yorkshire. The spot has always been popular for wild swimming, and on warm days it is often thronged with adventurous bathers lining up to dive from the mossy shelf into the deep plunge pool below. Nonetheless, the drop can be perilous – especially when the falls are in spate – and local legend

Lumb Fall in Crimsworth Dean near Hebden Bridge.

associates the scene with the suicide of a local beauty, whose unhappy phantom still stalks the vicinity.

Local tradition claims the girl was named Catherine and her father owned a number of farms in the vicinity – including Cross Ends, Stone Booth and Mold Grain. Two suitors sought her hand in marriage and the two eventually came to blows above Crimsworth Dean, where the old packhorse route between Hebden Bridge and Keighley skirts the edge of Shackleton Moor.

The two sustained mortal wounds in the fight and – because both were now considered murders – they were refused burial in consecrated ground. Instead, they were interred at the site of their conflict and a monument was raised to mark their resting place; two tapered slabs set upright into a stone base, each face incised with a crude cross. In actual fact, this is Abel Cross and although the

precise origin of this antiquity remains vague, it seems more likely to have been erected as a wayside cross to guide travellers over the moors sometime after the Middle Ages.

Meanwhile, Catherine blamed herself for the death of her two admirers. Some say she visited their graves every day and pined away beside them; others assert that she threw herself from the parapet of Lumb Bridge or hanged herself in a barn in Cross Ends. Her corpse is imagined to have been buried between the two shafts of Abel Cross and thereby between the men who died on her account.

These variants or 'allomotifs' are all united in their assertion that a spectral 'white lady', identified with Catherine's ghost, haunts the area around Cross Ends, Lumb Hole and Abel Cross in Crimsworth Dean. The romantic character of the legend suggests that the tale is entirely fictitious, but even if this is the

*Abel Cross above Crimsworth Dean.*

case, the white lady of Crimsworth Dean remains a strong tradition in its own right and paranormal phenomena has often been observed in the valley.

Gus and Tessa Smith of Stone Booth Farm (one of those supposedly once owned by Catherine's father) told the folklorist John Billingsley that they had witnessed anomalous lights on three occasions between 1984 and 1992. These orbs of luminescence had seemed to move along the western edge of the valley, tracing the route of the old packhorse road towards Coppy, then down Sunny Bank towards Lumb Hole. On one occasion, Tessa had even come within 10 yards of one near the ruin of Upper Sunny Bank.

Meanwhile, their son, Giles, claimed to have seen the 'white lady' moving past Upper Sunny Bank towards Coppy in April 1995. Like the experiences at Broadbottom Farm, these reports seem

to bear out the theory that geophysical phenomena known as earthlights might be responsible for many 'white lady' sightings across Britain. As John Billinglsey observes, Crimsworth Dean's geology is favourable for earthlights – thought to be the result of tectonic stress generating a piezoelectric effect in rocks with high quartz content.

Indeed, much of the Upper Calder Valley is extensively faulted and the dominant rock type – a sedimentary sandstone known as Millstone Grit – is rich in quartz. This fact has not been lost on paranormal researchers such as Paul Devereux and Jenny Randles who have suggested that a range of phenomena in the valley, including hauntings, faery legends and UFO sightings, may be attributable to its distinct geological features – a single phenomenon diversely interpreted according to the dominant belief framework of the witness.

## Blake Dean, Widdop

The moors that enclose the Upper Calder Valley are amongst the most remote and desolate in England. Travellers on the Widdop Road, which runs from Heptonstall Slack over the hills towards Colne in Lancashire, may be forgiven for thinking they have left civilisation behind entirely. But it was not always thus and the communities whose activities still scar these heights were once sufficient to justify their own churches and schools. These buildings may long since have lost their original purpose, but their austere presence endures.

Blake Dean is one such place. Now barely a hamlet, it is centred around the poetically named Meeting of the Waters – where Graining Water converges with Alcomden Water to flow down through Hardcastle Crags toward the Calder. The meeting of two streams is another strongly liminal point and perhaps it is not unusual that Blake Dean was considered in need of spiritual protection. A Baptist chapel was erected there in 1820 and thrived for some 120 years. It was eventually demolished in 1970, but its cemetery and Sunday school remain – the latter as a Scout hostel.

Despite the influence of its chapel, the vicinity of Blake Dean is reputed to be the haunt of a phantom known as the Green Lady. She has been seen stalking through the graveyard or riding a phantom horse down the valley, but always resplendent in a green velvet coat with pearl buttons and black leather riding boots. Her nocturnal perambulations are most strongly associated with New Year's Eve, although the only encounter whose date is recorded occurred around midsummer in 1953 and her presence remains the terror of Scouts staying at the hostel today.

The Green Lady's story was often told to travellers on the Widdop Road, by Midgley Barritt, who served as landlord at the nearby Packhorse Inn from 1915 until 1933. However, he had a reputation as a yarn-spinner and it is unclear to what extent he embellished the story. The legend as it is remembered today bears the hallmarks of a romantic gloss laid over a much older and more ambiguous tradition.

According to this version, the Green Lady's death was connected with the construction of the Walshaw Dean Reservoirs – a huge engineering project which demanded so much labour that an entire shanty town known as Dawson City was constructed outside Heptonstall to provide accommodation. Between 1900 and 1912 this pop-up slum housed up to 600 navvies at a time: enough people to justify the construction of a temporary hospital, library and mission church. Inevitably, however, it was despised by the locals as a den of lawlessness, alcoholism and disease.

Labour and materials were transported from Dawson City to the Walshaw site by a narrow-gauge railway constructed in 1901, which was forced to cross a trestle

*The packhorse bridge across Blake Dean at Widdop.*

bridge over Blake Dean. At 700ft across and more than 100ft high, the bridge towered above the Meeting of the Waters until it was demolished in 1912. Its stone footings can still be seen in Blake Dean today, near to an eddy in the Hebden Water known as Green Lady Pool – the name of which may be instructive.

Legend maintains that the Green Lady lived in a cottage near the chapel at Blake Dean during the early twentieth century and fell in love with one of the navvies working on the reservoirs. When construction was complete, he no longer needed to stay in Dawson City and spurned his local sweetheart, who then leapt to her death from the trestle bridge at Blake Dean, into Green Lady Pool below.

This is an all too familiar narrative in English ghost lore and its lack of particularity in details such as names may reflect its fictional nature. Equally, there seems to be no reason to invent such a story when a very real tragedy occurred at Blake Dean on 22 May 1909. Mrs Ada Harwood, a milliner from Hebden Bridge, was crossing the bridge with her family when the platform on which she was standing gave away and plunged her into the chasm below. Her nephew, George Arthur Smith, only survived by hanging from the railings until he could be rescued.

Neither scenario seems to account for the nature of the Green Lady of Blake Dean satisfactorily. Legends attached to ghosts such as these are often a recent superimposition on a much older belief. Folklorists have often observed that phantom ladies tend to haunt liminal locations – including pools, bridges, wells, cemeteries and ancient ruins – leading them to suggest that these spectres may

be a survival of much older animistic beliefs which credited such locations with their own tutelary spirit – a genius loci that evolved from daemon to faery to ghost with changing religious beliefs.

To the pre-modern mind, the Meeting of the Waters would've seemed a powerfully liminal point in its own right. However, it is also interesting that one elderly resident of Hebden Bridge recalls that in his youth, prehistoric earthworks could still be seen beside Green Lady Pool, adding yet another dimension of liminality to the area. Considered in such a context, the Green Lady stands not as the mere shade of some unfortunate local woman, but the spiritual personification of Blake Dean itself.

## Dale Street, Todmorden

Long-term residents of Todmorden will recall Dale Street as the former site of Carlton Buildings, a striking example of Victorian civic architecture which, for many years, housed the Todmorden Co-operative Society's flagship store. The society had been established by a group of local factory workers in 1846, only two years after the modern co-operative movement had been founded by the Rochdale Society of Equitable Pioneers.

They prospered over the following decades and their prestigious three-storied premises on Dale Street opened in 1883, complete with several departments, a library, refectory and assembly room. In 1908, the Dale Street Co-op became one of the first public buildings in Todmorden to install electric lighting and, during the 1920s and 1930s, the third-floor assembly room found popularity as a dance hall called the Astoria Ballroom.

However, like many co-operative movements nationally, the fortunes of the Todmorden society began to wane during the consumerist revolution of the 1950s. The Astoria Ballroom closed its doors in 1961 and only six years later a fire gutted the upper storeys, leaving them unusable. The retail departments continued to operate from the ground floor until 1995, when the society finally admitted defeat and abandoned Carlton Buildings.

*The former Co-op site on Dale Street in Todmorden.*

Following its closure, the property stood vacant for several years and as its dereliction grew, so did rumours that it was haunted. The local imagination began to populate its blank windows with barely glimpsed faces and purposeful shadows.

Shortly before the eventual demolition of the premises in 2000, local historian Bill Birch was escorted for a final look around by the site foreman who complained that a number of his team were reluctant to work in the cellars, citing strange draughts and an eerie atmosphere. But although the building was levelled as planned and modern residential blocks constructed in its place, sinister phenomena persisted.

In 2007, Yvonne and Ralph Blackman – tenants of one of the new flats on Dale Street – bought a commercial reproduction of a painting called 'A Quiet Forest' by Gerald Coulson from King's Mill in Burnley. A fairly superficial work, it portrays a stag stood in a shaft of sunlight penetrating a forest glade, and for three years the Blackman family noticed nothing else.

However, when they mounted the print on their living room wall in 2010, they began to discern another figure in the painting. Mrs Blackman told the

*Todmorden News*, 'I couldn't believe it when I first saw the girl's face in the picture. She's got dark hair but ... I've seen five different people; including a man and a girl. But I've seen evil too. All of a sudden it changed and really scared me; there's an evil man in there.'

Moreover, this incongruous manifestation seemed to morph identities and move about in the image – once more invoking the spectre of M.R. James's classic ghost story of 1904, *The Mezzotint*. Mrs Blackman felt sure that the girl's face was moving more prominently into the foreground and claimed that other people had confirmed her observations. Sadly, these independent witnesses are not identified or quoted, as is all too often the case.

The local press had little difficulty in connecting these uncanny experiences on the site of Carlton Buildings with a dismal murder committed on the premises in the heyday of the old Co-op. The victim was a 25-year-old woman named Clara Law – an employee of the store in 1891 – and conveniently an excellent fit for Mrs Blackman's dark-haired girl.

Clara's body was discovered in the Dale Street premises on the night of 3 August 1891 with her throat slit. As manager of the confectionery department, she had been working late and her absence had not initially been missed. Blame was directed at John William Halstead – assistant manager of the butcher's department and Clara's former fiancé – with whom she'd been conducting an affair despite his pledge to marry another. Earlier in the year, Clara had discovered that she was pregnant. Halstead had urged her to abort the child, and refused successive demands for marriage.

Despite the circumstantial evidence pointing toward Halstead, he maintained his innocence. However, the morning following an interview with the police, the young man threw himself in front of a train emerging from the eastern portal of the Horsfall Tunnel near his home at Eastwood. A suicide note in Halstead's pocket read:

> It appears to me they intend to swear my life away. It appears to me, although I am innocent, that they are all against me. She has been constantly trying to scandalize me, but this shall be final. Do not put any blame upon anyone; I will take it all myself …

The inquest into Clara's death, meanwhile, concluded several days later at the York Hotel in Todmorden. The coroner judged, 'We are of the opinion that the deceased, Clara Law, was murdered, but that there is not sufficient evidence to show by whom the wound in the throat which caused her death was inflicted.' More than a century after her death, the legacy of that injustice haunts the residents of Dale Street still.

## The Black Swan Hotel, Todmorden

Although the present building was entirely rebuilt in 1932, this pub on Burnley Road has been at the hub of Todmorden life for over two centuries. The Black Swan first opened as a hostelry in 1790, converted from a former carriers' warehouse; and during its early days – prior to the establishment of a police force in the borough – it conveniently housed the town lock-up. In recent years, the institution fell on hard times and closed for a short while, before reopening under the less historically resonant name, The Polished Knob.

Poltergeist phenomena beset the Black Swan between 1979 and 1982, following that common catalyst – renovation work. The licensees, Les and Kathleen Byram, reported a catalogue of incidents during their tenure, and whilst the activity followed a familiar pattern for pub hauntings, its severity was unusual.

Inevitably, taps on the barrels in the cellar regularly turned themselves off; sometimes in the course of a single shift and despite their locking mechanism. Heavy fire doors slammed shut in the absence of wind and the family dog was often seen to react with inexplicable hostility towards certain areas of the bar.

Glasses behaved badly, of course, but often in front of multiple witness, with a frequency and ferocity that was far from run-of-the-mill. Over the course of one night, several full pint glasses on the bar exploded, showering customers with shards and beer; whilst on another occasion – a Sunday lunchtime – a large party was just about to leave the pub when a tray of twenty empties they'd

*The Polished Knob, formerly the Black Swan Hotel, at Todmorden.*

left on the table shattered simultaneously and without any contact. The landlord stressed that he and his staff treated the glassware well, always allowing them to cool between washing and use.

After four years of living with the phenomena, the family had adopted a fairly stoic attitude towards it. Les told the *Todmorden News* in 1982, 'It's got to the stage now where we don't think about it. We just say "he's here again". I'll not have him moved unless he starts throwing things about.'

A couple who served as relief managers whilst the Byrams were on holiday were rather less sanguine, however. Along with regular customer, George Cryer, they were disturbed by the sound of heavy footsteps pounding through the ceiling above, although they were certain nobody was in the living quarters at the time. Mr Cryer recalled, 'I came in at night about 9.15 p.m. and … we heard footsteps coming across above our heads. Whatever it was it must

have been wearing size 20 boots … [The manager's] wife was terrified of going to bed that night.'

Regulars at the Black Swan began to speculate that these ghostly occurrences were the work of the pub's most notorious former customer: Miles Weatherill. Weatherhill was a local check-weaver who in 1868 committed one of the bloodiest murders the town has ever seen, which became a macabre sensation in Victorian society.

The previous year, Miles had met and fallen in love with Sarah Bell, who worked as a kitchen maid at the vicarage for Revd Anthony Plow. As she was only 16 and Miles was 22 the vicar disapproved of their relationship. When his attempts to prevent the couple from meeting failed, he dismissed Sarah from his service and she was forced to return to her home near Thirsk. Although Miles had previously been of good character, he fell into a black depression following Sarah's departure and began to drink heavily.

On the night of 2 March 1868, he had been imbibing at the Black Swan, from which he proceeded straight to the vicarage armed with four pistols and an axe. He attacked members of the household without compunction: the nursery maid, Jane Smith, was killed outright by a pistol shot; Revd Plow and his 6-week-old daughter, Hilda Katherine, were mortally wounded; and Harriet Plow, the vicar's wife, was so severely beaten and traumatised that she only clung to life for a year following the incident.

Miles Weatherhill did not try to evade arrest and he was charged with murder at Manchester Assizes on 20 March. He was hanged alongside another murderer beneath the walls of New Bailey Gaol at 8 a.m. on 4 April 1868. The tragedy had so captured the public interest that several thousand people gathered at the scaffold to watch what turned out to be the last public execution in Manchester.

Although the Victorian vicarage in which the murders occurred is now privately owned, its macabre reputation still endures in Todmorden and local tradition holds that the ghostly face of a young woman can sometimes be seen staring from the windows – doubtless believed to be the visage of poor Jane Smith still bound to the scene of her grievous fate.

Nor is it a surprise to find the name of Miles Weatherill attached to the anonymous poltergeist at the Black Swan Hotel. As the folklorist Gillian Bennett observes of such enigmatic hauntings, 'The havoc they wreak after their death … gets explained by the havoc of their living or dying. Either they are assumed to have had a malice so intense that it cannot die, or they are assumed to have had a death so cruel that the death itself cannot die.' Miles Weatherill may only have spent a little time in the pub, but his name so snugly fits the narrative conventions that popular discourse demands.

## The Fielden Centre, Todmorden

This community centre on the far edge of Centre Vale Park is just one of the many institutions in Todmorden to bear the Fielden name, commemorating a family of wealthy industrialists who are inexorably linked with the development of the town in the nineteenth century. Despite his temper and arrogance earning him the nickname 'Black Sam', Samuel Fielden was a prodigious philanthropist and he paid for the construction of Centre Vale Elementary School in 1872. This establishment provided an education for nearly 400 children, under the leadership of his wife, Sarah, a nationally respected educationalist.

Her son, John Ashton Fielden, had little interest in the town, which he dismissed as 'damp, dirty and dull'. As such, he sold the school to the Todmorden Corporation following his mother's retirement in 1896, and it subsequently became the Fielden School of Art for many years. In the 1950s it provided classrooms for a newly opened Todmorden Secondary School, but when this merged with the local grammar school to become Todmorden High School in 1978, it gradually fell into disuse. A charitable organisation purchased the lease in 1997 and extensively renovated the almost-derelict building, converting it into a successful community and arts centre.

Rumours of a haunting at the Fielden Centre seem to have arisen during the

*The Fielden Centre at Todmorden.*

1950s and clung to its austere Victorian edifice through decades of dilapidation. Whilst raising funds for the renovation, the Fielden Centre Association encountered many local residents who had spent time in the building during its use by Todmorden Secondary School and a number attested to its uncanny reputation. Committee member Sarah Pennie told a local newspaper, 'Almost all the ex-pupils and teachers we spoke to … remember the building as cold, damp and sometimes haunted.'

Mrs Pennie also noted, 'Various caretakers say they have seen the ghost of a woman believed to be Mrs Fielden. She is reported to have been seen at the door of the hall and in another part of the building used as an office.' Although she had seen nothing herself, Pennie claimed the building was plagued by a phantom odour reminiscent of disinfectants such as carbolic acid – a smell closely associated with the Victorian schoolroom.

It is perhaps unsurprising that the ghost of Sarah Jane Fielden should remain attached to the Fielden Centre when she is enshrined in its very name. To those who recall the 'cold and damp' school in the 1950s and its subsequent slide into dereliction, her unquiet spirit becomes a tragic personification of its decay: the empty, crumbling building represented a betrayal or perversion of its function. It is perhaps equally unsurprising that her ghost has not been seen since the renovation – restoring the building to community use, imbuing it with vitality, exorcises such phantasms more effectively than any priest.

## The Sour Hall, Todmorden

Located over 1,000ft above sea level on the bleak, windswept plateau of Todmorden Moor, the building known as the Sour Hall (as distinct from

The Sour Hall on the moors above Todmorden.

Sourhall, the surrounding hamlet) was constructed sometime in the eighteenth century. Over the years it has operated as the Dog & Partridge, Sour Hall Country Club and the Country Friends Inn, but at the time of writing its doors were closed and future uncertain. In such straitened times for the pub industry, its uniquely remote situation could not have helped trade. Even the roads here remain barely more than tracks.

At the turn of the millennium, however, the Sour Hall was still serving under its unadorned moniker and the license had just been taken on by two local businessmen, Colin Boswell and Fred Trafford. Eighteen months later, in May 2001, Boswell told the local press that he feared they'd acquired more than just the fixtures and fittings.

He reported a typical litany of poltergeist activity in the moorland pub: doors opening and closing of their own accord, lights switching on and off without agency, cold spots and mysterious noises. A regular customer's dog would shrink from a certain corner of the bar and, on one occasion, a young barmaid was showered with glass when stacked glasses flew off the shelves towards her.

Boswell experienced most of the phenomena himself, and despite his business partner's scepticism, he engaged the veteran Todmorden clairvoyant, Katavia Hall, to 'cleanse' the building. After she'd spent half a day performing various rituals around the pub – allegedly identifying three restless spirits in the process – Boswell seemed satisfied. 'It has definitely calmed down since then,' he told a journalist several months later. 'All the cold spots disappeared and the banging stopped – we were able to turn the central heating down.'

It is not clear exactly what sort of spirits Ms Hall distinguished, but the proximity of a former fever hospital is difficult to ignore. For until 1949, a row of cottages just across the lane from the pub originally housed the Todmorden & District Authority Joint Hospital for Infectious Disease; or more pithily – Sourhall Isolation Hospital.

The hospital opened with room for sixteen patients following a local smallpox epidemic in 1874, and over the years, its remit was extended to treat typhoid, diphtheria and scarlatina. The institution was enlarged in 1907, but the decline of such diseases in Britain during the twentieth century – thanks largely to medical advances and improved sanitation – ultimately led to its closure, after which the building was converted into private residences.

Nonetheless, numerous fatalities occurred at the hospital in its early days: for instance, John Fielden Haight, a farmer from Walsden, died in 1886; followed by Benjamin Swire of Shade and Henry Wilkinson of Lydgate in 1888 – all from typhoid fever. Were these unfortunate souls confined to the lonely hamlet of Sourhall even in death, driven to seek solace from desolation of the moor within the walls of the old Dog & Partridge Inn?

# BIBLIOGRAPHY

## Books

Ahier, Philip, *Legends & Traditions of Huddersfield & its District* (Huddersfield: The Advertister Press, 1994)

Bennett, Paul, *The Old Stones of Elmet* (Milverton: Capall Bann Publishing, 2001)

Billingsley, John, *Stony Gaze: Investigating Celtic & Other Stone Head* (Milverton: Capall Bann Publishing, 1998)

Billingsley, John (ed.), *Aspects of Calderdale* (Barnsley: Wharncliffe Books, 2002)

Billingsley, John, *Folk Tales from Calderdale Vol. 1* (Hebden Bridge: Northern Earth, 2007)

Billingsley, John, *The Mixenden Treasure* (Hebden Bridge: Northern Earth, 2009)

Billinglsey, John, *West Yorkshire Folk Tales* (Stroud: The History Press, 2010)

Billinglsey, John, *Hood, Head & Hag: Further Folk Tales from Calderdale* (Hebden Bridge: Northern Earth, 2011)

Campbell, Marie, *Strange World of the Brontës* (Wilmslow: Sigma Leisure, 2001)

Crabtree, John, *A Concise History of the Parish & Vicarage of Halifax* (Halifax: Hartley & Walker, 1836)

Drinkall, Margaret, *Halifax Murders* (Stroud: The History Press, 2013)

Gee, Stephen, *Halifax Pubs Volume 1* (Stroud: The History Press, 2008)

Gee, Stephen, *Halifax Pubs Volume 2* (Stroud: Amberley Publishing, 2011)

Goss, Michael, 'The Halifax Slasher' (London: *Fortean Times*, 1987)

Hamerton, Lucy, *Olde Eland* (Unknown: Gledhill, 1901)

Hughes, Glyn, *Millstone Grit* (Newton Abbot: Readers Union Ltd, 1975)

Illingworth, Jean, *Growing up in Sowerby & More* (Hebden Bridge: The Book Case, 2008)

Lofthouse, Jessica, *North Country Folklore* (London: Robert Hale & Company, 1976)

Marsh, John, *Clip a Bright Guinea: Yorkshire Coiners of the Eighteenth Century* (Skipton: Dalesman Publishing, 1990)

Midgeley, Samuel, *Halifax & its Gibbet Law Placed In Its True Light* (Halifax: William Bentley, 1761)

Owens, Andy, *Yorkshire Stories of the Supernatural* (Newbury: Countryside Books, 1999)

Owens, Andy, *Haunted Places of Yorkshire* (Newbury: Countryside Books, 2005)

Owens, Andy, *Paranormal West Yorkshire* (Stroud: The History Press, 2008)

Parker, James, *Illustrated Rambles from Hipperholme to Tong* (Bradford: Percy Lund, Humphries & Co. Ltd, 1904)

Porritt, Arthur, *It Happened Here: Volumes 1–3* (Unknown: Weardale Press, 1955–69)

Rinder, Albert, *A History of Elland* (Unknown, 1987)

Roberts, Andy, *Ghosts & Legends of Yorkshire* (Norwich: Jarrold Publishing, 1992)

Roberts, Kai, *Folklore of Yorkshire* (Stroud: The History Press, 2013)

Turner, Joseph Horsfall, *History of Brighouse, Rastrick & Hipperholme* (Halifax: T. Harrison, 1893)

Wade, Stephen, *Foul Deeds & Suspicious Deaths in & around Halifax* (Barnsley: Wharncliffe Books, 2004)

Wade, Stephen, *Hauntings in Yorkshire* (Wellington: Halsgrove, 2008)

Watson, John, *History of Antiquities of the Parish of Halifax in Yorkshire* (Halifax: Lowdnes, 1775)

Weatherhead, Paul, *Weird Calderdale* (Hebden Bridge: Tom Bell Publishing, 2005)

Whitaker, Terence, *Yorkshire Ghosts & Legends* (London: Harper Collins Publishers Ltd, 1983)

Wright, Thomas, *The Antiquities of the Town of Halifax in Yorkshire* (Halifax: J. Lister, 1738)

## Periodicals

*Brighouse Echo*
*Calderdale News*
*The Dalesman*
*Halifax Evening Courier*
*Halifax Guardian*
*Hebden Bridge Times*
*Milltown Memories*
*Northern Earth*
*Transactions of the Halifax Antiquarian Society*
*Todmorden News*
*Yorkshire Folklore Journal*
*Yorkshire Notes & Queries*

Visit our website and discover thousands of other History Press books.

**www.thehistorypress.co.uk**

Lightning Source UK Ltd.
Milton Keynes UK
UKOW04f1332110614

233215UK00004B/9/P

9 780750 96006